Climate Ch

By David Phillips

Table of Contents

Dedication

I have many people to thank in the writing of this book.

Its inspiration came from Peter Kendall who was kind enough to complement a pamphlet I produced.

My critic and editor Sarah Pasteur is an inspirational mentor and a friend to my wife who has tolerated many days of silence from her spouse. Some may think this is a good thing!

Synopsis

Housing has yet to cope. Climate Change is murderous. Global Warming has changed the world. Here is the manifesto for homes to face up to the Global Warming menace and for people to live in safe and healthy housing.

Sometimes acerbic, fully researched, and highly critical of institutional blunders, this book offers fresh insights and creative solutions to meet the three big issues of the day.

It identifies and pours scorn on wasted efforts, costing the population dear and turns a spotlight on poorly thought through rambling regulations. Here is a manifesto to create positive opportunities in a trillion pound sector. And then, as if by magic, it shows how it can cost the Treasury nothing.

About the Author

A political organiser in the Thatcher era, a corporate affairs director, journalist and academic.

David was a prolific industrial journalist to the material handling press and contributed to The Engineer, The Times and Daily Telegraph. He is the author of several technical books on the internet and online relationship management.

He has lectured across Europe and is a widely published academic author.

He is a Fellow of the Chartered Institute of Public Relations.

Chapter 1: Introduction

Housing has yet to cope. Climate is a threat. Change is coming. This book looks at British house building, renewing and refurbishment against the twin threats of Global Warming and Climate Change.

It is beyond imagination to discover: "One roadblock is that policy is separated into different departments in government. Previously, electricity regulations were different from gas regulations, which were different from heat and transport… going forward all of those boundaries are going to become really blurred," warns Dr Madeleine Morris, "they need to take a whole-system view." These are crises, not rounds of inter-department arm wrestling.

Here is an attempt to discover all the separate influencers and ally them with a range of well-informed contributors who help us understand and resolve problems and threats.

The 2022 Queen's Speech promised further muddle, and HM Secretary of State, Micheal Gove's brainwaves that came to him in the bath, like the Social Housing Regulation Bill, Levelling Up and Regeneration Bill, Energy Security Bill and Public Order Bill all of which miss the point of integrated building and renovating for the future. Each is OK but there is not even a dotted line between them.

Friederike Otto at Imperial College London, says "I think we can very confidently now say that every heatwave that is occurring today has been made more intense and more likely because of Climate Change. There is no doubt that Climate Change is really an absolute game changer when it comes to heatwaves."

Over the next five years, more action is essential to keep pace with the rising risks facing UK housing.

Homes are suffering increased problems due to global warming and the resultant frequency and severity of Climate Change.

Politically, people are leaning towards improved protection and mitigation of Climate Change and it's now a significant influence. And belief in human-created Climate Change which ranks third among the most critical issues for the population at large. YouGov opinion polls also show Climate Change as a key concern among electors and 80% of the adult population think of housing as an issue.

In five years, 570,000 new homes were built between 2016 and 2021. Mostly these new homes are not Climate Change resilient. Current policies throw a woolly insulation blanket over houses (new and old) and call it renovation, refurbishment or global warming mitigation and when the days pass with temperatures close to, or above, 40°C it becomes apparent that the need was for Climate Change mitigation is a much bigger and life-threatening problem.

Occupants are at risk of overheating in their homes (there are still an estimated two thousand heat-related deaths per year and increasing). Household heating in winter is very likely to decrease due to warmer winters, and summer air conditioning demand will grow.

Fire is now a big problem and a threat to houses and much more.

Flooding is already a severe risk to UK houses. It's not funny. Flooded housing causes long-term and severe impacts on mental health and wellbeing, not to mention property damage. This risk is already high, with 1.9 million people across all areas of the UK at risk. Flooding from either river, coastal or surface water flooding will get worse, say the experts.

Buildings are affected by dampness due to flooding and heavy rain, structural damage due to high winds and subsidence caused.

Drought is an issue for one in five people. Can insurance cover the cost? Can people stand dumping sodden heirlooms and carpets? Do floods affect mental health - you bet.

A higher incidence of water scarcity is also a real threat with the prospect of interruptions to housing water supply. Lack of water causes health, social and economic impacts, particularly for vulnerable households.

Poor internal air quality costs the NHS £billions and gets a passing mention about mould and yet cars pass by shedding nanoparticles, black carbon, polycyclic hydrocarbons, nitrogen oxides and more into houses sickening children and the elderly inside.

Against this scary landscape, there is no time to equivocate, and there is a need for a comprehensive joined up modern housing manifesto.

It's time to use modern techniques, create enough homes, remove carbuncle building (notably blighting villages so much admired by the money spending tourists) and cut back on the builders' practice of creating a mud puddle ahead of laying Co2 emitting concrete and bricks.

It is time that proper sanctions be applied to those responsible.

The book shows how to increase national house building productivity by slaying rampant speculation. It invites the reader to imagine cutting the national debt by repurposing slums and reigning in wasteful handouts by munificent Chancellors of the Exchequer.

Why should homes not generate new energy sources for 300,000 houses per year and power their owners' homes and electric cars (EVs) for free?

In July 2022, Britain lived through a record-breaking 40.3°C heatwave an unprecedented and unexpected temperature. Here we look at how housing can mitigate current and impending Climate Change threats in houses with a lifespan of more than 30 years and, at the same time, add to the nation's efforts to manage Global Warming.

Among so many promises is the view that health service costs and social care needs require better housing management and can offer good health to so many suffering from life in dying buildings.

Housing has not changed much in a generation. Gas, electricity, damp proofing, and insulation were installed when Marty Quant invented the miniskirt—falling construction volumes, notably by public authorities, after the rush to build post-war 'Homes for Heros' meant, for ordinary people, a growing level of housing debt and fewer houses to rent. The Thatcherite attempt to solve the problem was to create a 'property-owning democracy' and sales of local council homes.

Barratt Homes, the UK's biggest builder, announced in October 2021 that it was going to build a "flagship zero-carbon concept home. All of its new homes will be zero carbon from 2030. This is to be welcomed especially because it is well thought through. Barratt may be the biggest builder, but there are many more builders needing to come up to the mark soon. Ten years in a crisis is a long time.

There is a housing shortage and a Climate Change threat. In that time, 20,000 people will die just from heat waves.

Over the years, house prices in the UK have rocketed. So much so, it's hard to imagine a time when buying a new home costs less than £3,000. If you could afford to buy a home after the war, it was probably brand new. That was around £65,224 in today's money, and the average salary was roughly the equivalent of £339 per week.

The electric fire, the washing machine and the humble fish finger were life-changing inventions of the era. Within a decade, most homes in the UK had electricity, a fridge, an electric cooker, a telephone and a black and white TV.

Now, colour TV, home computing and printing with networked internet wifi that can remotely control the washing-up machine, carpet cleaner, lawn mower and central heating are now commonplace but in a house costing, on average, more than a quarter of a million pounds. Somehow these assets are funded from the annual average wage of £30,000.

Thus we have a shrinking supply of houses at prices many cannot afford. Many people and families are falling below their ability and the ability of public services, and often charitable institutions, to put a roof over the head of so many households.

Here then, are the ingredients of the crisis and we have to find ways of creating homes for all the population, including those living in dingy and damp homes.

As if one crisis was not enough, the realisation of the impending crisis caused by global warming has crept upon us.

Global warming sets the backdrop to all that has to be achieved to solve the housing crisis.

Global warming has an evil twin: Climate Change.

Driven by $Co2$ and methane production, Climate Change is a huge cloud hanging over the homes of all of us. It brings evermore intensive heat waves, cold, storms, floods and fires more frequently than ever before.

Persistent high-pressure "blocking" weather systems bring clear, dry conditions for many days or weeks in the northern hemisphere and are evident as high pressure and an absence of wind.

Such events (like the ones in 2022) are 17% more likely due to Climate Change. It means that the windmills will stop more often in winter and there will be temporary shortages of green electricity.

In the face of Global Warming, use of concrete, brick, and PVC have remained contributors to such disasters. They are, of course, among the most environmentally damaging materials. They remain evident in hundreds of thousands of new houses built every year.

A home should be an affordable, spacious refuge from Climate Change. A home office is a place for families to take advantage of the internet and the Meta Universe and thrive for a generation. Later in this book, we look at these great alternatives and provide references to offer wider perspectives to the reader.

The UK housing industry can easily commit to development that includes added green energy for 600,000 houses over the next three years. Its efforts can make housing a productive part of the economy and an early market to support world-leading technologies. It can be new jobs, new assets and a bonus in national productivity.

It can also commit to solving a considerable part of the Social Care shortfall, creating supportive accommodation for the elderly and frail and upwards of 25,000 new dwellings for the homeless and challenged families in Britain.

These are among the solutions outlined in this book. There are more.

It makes sense for new builds to mitigate rapidly growing storms, floods and droughts (yes… at no cost to the Treasury).

In addition to solar panels, there are new and even more flexible solutions to harvesting light. Vertical windmills are an evolving source of power generation; even roads can make houses independent of the grid. Imagine free fuel for the car, drought-free water supply for the garden, free electricity, free heating and cooling and subsequent generation and reliable WiFi.

A population leaning towards improved protection and mitigation of global warming and local Climate Change is a significant political influence. It ranks third among the most critical issues for the British population at large.

Building a house in modules in one or more (already available) factories in a couple of weeks is needed and possible. Taking the modules to the site for completion within a week is commonly achieved. These achievements could be called building without the bla bla bla!

The majority of homes are old and need updating. Many are derelict and need re-purposing. A considerable number of houses are empty, and there is the issue of underused holiday homes. Using more modern and environmentally friendly materials, devices and capabilities is necessary. Ramping up output from hundreds to thousands is not a big issue if the incentive and political leadership are there. These homes are not as expensive to produce as the traditional glutenous and muddy building site competition.

New skills and career changes will be part of the deal, and up-skilling and growth in this sector (with the prospect of an economic effect that will increase national productivity) is now on the cards.

Many new options are possible. Solar, wind, and rain harvesting have a multiplier effect (one extra KW from each house adds up to an extra 300,000 KW each year). Meanwhile, quality control in the house construction factories can and should be to a much higher standard (and is much easier to police and resolve). Much of the housing crisis can be resolved in factories to meet the emerging 'Passive House' standards.

These issues and solutions are a radical but significant opportunity for builders, the building industry and estate managers. Here we see a competitive advantage, more stable markets, enhanced margins and a stable order book well into the future.

The modern home can also be a refuge from diseases and air pollution such as the common cold, flu, Covid19, pollen, traffic pollutants and more. Why not save the NHS £157 million and rising, each year just by building better, virus-free homes? Filtered air and heat exchange makes this possible.

Homes can be built for communities that inter-alia help provide social care and reduce costs.

The legacy of these and many more proposals will be felt for the life of the newly built houses lasting more than 50 years.

Often, the policy solutions cut across government department boundaries and between governments nationally and locally. These proposals do the same. In a housing crisis, some decisions need to override many impediments to success. Institutions that impede progress are both antisocial and economically damaging.

Policing can be built into housing and even drug running can be automatically sniffed out 24/7.

As a nation, we want to build 300,000 homes per year. Individually each house can contribute small gains. For example, the generation of an extra kilowatt of electricity submitted to the national grid is a mere nothing. But 300,000 kilowatts is a lot. Ten kilowatts per day from so many houses, with each house generating for their own needs as well, is, potentially, a massive contribution to the economy and releases a lot of power for other uses (e.g. domestic hydrogen production). The national multiplier effect is very significant. Such ideas offer a long-term national productivity gain and can be implemented in months not years.

The Housing Ministry needs powers to get things moving and be held responsible for resolving sluggish delivery. This applies to local governments as well. There will be calls for the construction industry to make radical contributions.

We all face the problem that someone has to bear the cost, and it can't all be the government. Here, we look at some solutions that bring both financial benefit and environmental solutions together. Slashing the schemes and machinations surrounding housing in the UK with their labyrinthine bureaucracy will reduce the cost of Treasury involvement.

Thinking about how the economy can live with this expensive approach to building is complex, and an inflation-proof concept has to be considered too.

At the same time, there will be a need to rethink housing as a concept in a changing climate and at the same time help in the provision of social care.

Nothing can be quite as radical as turning a house into a domestic revenue stream.

Sources and Reference Works Cited

Passivhaus Institut, https://passivehouse.com/. Accessed 15 May 2022.

"Average weekly earnings in Great Britain: November 2021." Average weekly earnings in Great Britain - Office for National Statistics, 16 November 2021, https://www.ons.gov.uk/employmentandlabourmarket/peopleinwork/employmentandemployeetypes/bulletins/average weeklyearningsi ngreatbritain/november2021. Accessed 13 May 2022.

"Barratt Developments launches the Z House: a flagship zero carbon concept home." Barratt Developments Plc, 25 October 2021, https://www.barrattdevelopments.co.uk/media/media-releases/pr-2 021/pr-25-10-2021. Accessed 13 May 2022.

Gibson, Scott. "Balanced Whole-House Ventilation - GreenBuildingAdvisor." Green Building Advisor, 8 October 2021, https://www.greenbuildingadvisor.com/article/balanced-whole-hou se-ventilation. Accessed 15 May 2022.

Hassan, Jennifer. "Greta Thunberg says blah blah blah during climate speech at Italy's Youth4Change." The Washington Post, 29 September 2021, https://www.washingtonpost.com/climate environment/2021/09/29/great-thunberg-leaders-blah-blah-blah/. Accessed 13 May 2022.

Hassan, Jennifer. "Greta Thunberg says blah blah blah during climate speech at Italy's Youth4Change." The Washington Post, 29 September2021, https://www.washingtonpost.com/climate-environment/2021/09/29/great-thunberg-leaders-blah-blah-blah/. Accessed 15 May 2022.

"History of house prices in Britain." SunLife, 30 June 2021, https://www.sunlife.co.uk/articles-guides/your-money/the-price-of- a-home-in-britain-then-and-n ow/. Accessed 13 May 2022.

"Legal & General Research Reveals Deepening Housing Crisis."Property Notify, 21 October 2021, https://www.propertynotify.co.uk/news/legal-general research-reve als-deepening-housing-crisis/. Accessed 15 May 2022.

Mehta, Amar. "UK weather: New Year's Eve could be mildest on record as temperatures expected to reach 15C, the Met Office says." Sky News, 28 December 2021, https://news.sky.com/story/uk-weather-new-years-eve-could-be-mi ldest-on-record-as-temperatur es-expected-to-reach-15c-the-met-office-says-12504593. Accessed 13 May 2022.

O'Hare, Ryan. "Air pollution in England could cost as much as

£5.3 billion by 2035 | Imperial News." Imperial College London, 22 May 2018,

https://www.imperial.ac.uk/news/186406/air-pollution-england-cou ld-cost-much/. Accessed 15 May 2022.

"Recent progress of efficient flexible solar cells based on nanostructures." Journal of Semiconductors,

http://www.jos.ac.cn/article/id/3ed0e42d-0632-4830-8b47 4f09f1a 2780a?viewType=HTML. Accessed 13 May 2022.

"Sector Briefings." UK Climate Risk,

https://www.ukclimaterisk.org/independent-assessment-ccra3/brief

ings/. Accessed 13 May 2022.

"Sector Briefings." UK Climate Risk,

https://www.ukclimaterisk.org/independent-assessment-ccra3/brief ings/. Accessed 13 May 2022.

Spyro, Steph. "Public concern on green issues at highest level, poll finds." Daily Express, 10 November 2021,

https://www.express.co.uk/news/nature/1519431/cop26-green-issu es-public-concern-highest-level-poll. Accessed 13 May 2022.

"Stalled weather patterns will get bigger due to Climate Change: Relationship between jet stream, atmospheric

blocking events." ScienceDaily, 13 November 2019,
https://www.sciencedaily.com/releases/2019/11/191113075
107.htm

. Accessed 13 May 2022. Stevens, John. "Rishi Sunak is to
announce cash for new houses on brownfield land." Daily
Mail, 24 October 2021,

https://www.dailymail.co.uk/news/article-10126429/Rishi-
Sunak-a nnounce-cash-injection-tens-t

housands-new-houses-brownfield-land.html. Accessed 13
May 2022.

"UK struggling to keep pace with Climate Change
impacts." Climate Change Committee, 16 June 2021,

https://www.theccc.org.uk/2021/06/16/uk-struggling-to-
keep-pace- with-climate-change-impacts/. Accessed 13
May 2022.

"A vertical axis wind turbine that doesn't need the
prevailing wind! How do they do that?" YouTube, 18 April
2021, https://www.youtube.com/watch?v=gcSnwW5v3f8.
Accessed 13

May 2022.

Warrington, James, et al. "FTSE 100 hits highest level for
almost two years." The Telegraph, 17 January 2022,

https://www.telegraph.co.uk/business/2022/01/17/ftse-100-
markets

-live-news-shares-interest-energy/. Accessed 13 May 2022.

"What is Wi-Fi 7 and When Will We Have It? — Geekabit Wi-Fi."

Geekabit, 24 February 2022,

https://geekabit.co.uk/2022/02/24/wi-fi-7-will-it/.

Accessed 13

May 2022.

"The wrong kind of rain: why Britain is not as wet as we think."

National Geographic, 26 May 2021,

https://www.nationalgeographic.co.uk/environment-and-conservati on/2021/05/the-wrong-kind-of-rain-why-britain-is-not-as-wet-as-w e-think. Accessed 13 May 2022.

Chapter 2: Global Warming and Homes

Nearly a quarter of the world's population experienced a record hot year in 2021. A year later the UK had record breaking temperatures, fires and drought and all that before the school summer holidays.

Globally, the extraordinary weather events are a catalogue of deadly proportions and, from a Sky News article, something like a wake-up call close to an environmental armageddon.

Building houses to the current standards (with a few exceptions) just add to the problem of environmental damage (Buildings generate nearly 40% of annual global CO_2 emission). Its use of resources and energy needs to be addressed. But, additionally, there is a need for restoring and maintaining older properties with similar demands.

Global warming has an evil twin: Climate Change.

Climate Change sets the backdrop to all that has to be done to solve the housing crisis.

It is time to ask whether we are doing enough and what more we can do. The UN secretary general, António Guterres, said some governments and businesses were "lying" in claiming to be on track for 1.5 degree centigrade. In a strongly worded rebuke, he warned: "Some government and business leaders are saying one thing – but doing another. Simply put, they are lying. And the results will be catastrophic."

Driven by CO2 and Methane production, global warming is a huge cloud hanging over the homes of us all. Climate Change is to bring ever more intensive heat waves, cold, storms, floods, fires and even winter droughts more frequently than ever before. Frequency and ferocity mark out these Climate Change events.

So-called "blocking events" in the northern hemisphere are evident as high pressure shows up as an absence of wind.

These events will increase by as much as 17% due to Climate Change. It means that the windmills are going to stop more often in winter as well as summer and there will be a shortage of green electricity unless we act now.

In the face of global warming, concrete, brick and PVC have remained major contributors to such disasters. They are, of course, among the most environmentally damaging materials and yet remain evident in hundreds of thousands of new houses built every year.

Professor Betts, a member of the University of Exeter's Global Systems Institute, said: "We are heating the global climate by causing greenhouse gasses to build up in the atmosphere. Further change is already locked-in so we urgently need to prepare for that3".

Can action taken now resolve or mitigate the impact of Global Warming and Climate Change?

In a YouGov poll in mid-2021, 59% of people said that we are "still able to avoid the worst effects of Climate Change but it would need a drastic change in the steps taken to tackle it". But 16% thought we are already too late and 40% are fairly frightened by the prospect.

The construction sector has to make its contribution or face severe criticism from the majority of the population.

"If every person on the planet were to consume resources as an average European, then we would need the resources of 2 planets now and 6 planets by 2050 to support our society and economy. This level of overconsumption is obviously not sustainable."

Concrete, bricks, tiles, roadways and diesel-powered site machinery are planet robbers.

Plaster, new wiring, old fashioned light bulbs, insulation and efficient heating are but a few elements that have to rise up our consciousness from now on.

Construction and renovation produce CO_2 by the tonne and consume huge levels of unusable and seldom recycled resources. The ground once absorbed rainwater and fixed greenhouse gases but is now covered in impermeable asphalt and concrete. So-called 'energy efficient new buildings produce 1.45 tonnes of CO_2 per year and deliver vast ammounts into the atmosphere according to the Experimental Official Statistics based on Energy Performance Certificates (EPC) per annum.

There are alternatives to concrete such as Hempcrete and Concretene (among others) and research into alternative materials is to be found all over the world.

We still accept that building a house will generate 80 tonnes of CO_2 (for a cottage with two bedrooms upstairs and two reception rooms, and a kitchen downstairs). Each Member of Parliament should know that about 43 tonnes of CO_2 are dumped on the world by each of their constituents annually. A really good briefing by the UK Health Alliance is worth reading to put the Global Warming imperative into context.

Efforts to adapt the UK's housing stock to the impacts of the changing climate: for higher average temperatures, flooding and water scarcity, are also lagging far behind what is needed to keep us safe and comfortable, even as these Climate Change risks grow.

Around 4.5 million homes overheat, even in cool summers; 1.8 million people live in areas at significant risk of flooding.

Average UK water consumption is higher than in many other European countries. Distributed water purification at house or street level is becoming a practical opportunity.

Removing a large part of the need for massive collection and purification infrastructure is a welcome alternative and will reduce the loss of water from a national crisis of mains water leaks.

Cost-effective measures to adapt the UK housing stock are not being rolled out at anywhere near the required level.

In its 2021 report 'UK housing: Fit for the future?' the Committee on Climate Change (CCC) warned that the UK's legally-binding Climate Change targets will not be met without the near-complete elimination of greenhouse gas emissions from UK buildings. The report finds that emission reductions from the UK's 29 million homes have stalled, while energy use in homes – which accounts for 14% of total UK emissions – increased between 2016 and 2017.

In the United Kingdom, renewable energy generation will need to increase by 50% by 2025 if the country is to reach its climate and energy targets.

With this in mind, a close examination of the UK Climate Risk report, an independent report to government published in early 2022, is important. This assessment takes a look forward 50 years (and beyond) being the minimum projection for the life of houses built and renovated in the next months.

It also notes that although the Paris Agreement commits the nations of the world to limit global warming to well below 2°C above pre-industrial levels and pursue efforts to limit warming to 1.5°C, projections consistent with policies currently in place worldwide imply warming of between approximately 2°C and 5°C by the end of this century depending on the rate of greenhouse gas emissions and the response of the climate system to these emissions. This will further increase the shifts in weather patterns and extremes, further increasing mortal risks to people and biodiversity, with higher warming leading to greater risks.

Since this report was published the 'wind drought' of winter 2021/2 has reduced electricity from wind turbines by 17%. Shifts in weather patterns sometimes come as a surprise.

Around 1.8 million people in the UK already live in areas of significant flood risk. If the frequent occurrence of major flooding events continues – which it has done in the UK nearly every year since 2007 – it is estimated that the number of homes at risk of flooding will rise by 40% to 2.6 million in as little as 20 years.

The UK Government is required by the Climate Change Act 2008 to conduct such an assessment every five years to inform the National Adaptation Plans for England, Scotland, Wales and Northern Ireland. This is the third such national assessment and the second time the Government has asked its independent advisers, the Climate Change Committee, to prepare the initial Independent Assessment.

It reports that "Action to improve the nation's resilience is failing to keep pace with the impacts of a warming planet and increasing climate risks facing the UK."

The World Economic Forum (WEF) has taken an interest in the energy used in buildings. In Europe alone, it notes, more than 220 million existing buildings – or 75% of the building stock – are energy-inefficient, with many relying on fossil fuels for heating and cooling.

European analysis from their System Value initiative shows that a 20% shift in heating towards heat pump applications running on clean electricity would reduce CO_2 emissions by 9%. Coupled with smart solutions, it could save €3 billion in human health benefits from decreased air pollution between now and 2030. Bear in mind that any building constructed today will be around for the next 50 years or more – so ensuring that new buildings are green and those existing buildings are decarbonized, is key to our efforts to combat Climate Change.

There are some other imperatives.

In 2020, Drax, one of the biggest power stations in Europe generated 11% of the UK's renewable power - enough for four million homes. It is using wood pellets from the USA instead of local coal. The climate think tank,

Ember, calculates that the power station is now the UK's single largest source of carbon dioxide. According to the think tank Chatham House, wood pellets from the US burnt in the UK generated 13-16 million tonnes of CO_2 emissions in 2019 - equivalent to the emissions from 6-7 million cars. Greenwash is dangerous.

As a nation, we want to build over 300,000 homes per year. As mentioned above, individually each house can contribute small gains. The production of 300,000 kilowatts from new UK houses is as big as a North Sea wind farm. Twelve kilowatts per day from so many houses with each house generating for their own needs, including an electric car as well, is, potentially, also a huge contribution to the economy. It will release a lot of power for other uses (e.g. hydrogen production). The national multiplier effect is very significant. Such ideas offer a long-term national productivity gain.

This alternative source is important because in recent years the yield from wind power has dropped.

Renewable generation in the last quarter 2021 fell 17% year-over-year to 24.3 TWh, a four-year low. It was hit by unfavourable weather, in particular, the slowest wind speeds in the current century (wind was not considered in the Climate Change risk in the CCC report). This sounds like global warming upsetting weather assumptions and thus renewable power solutions all over again.

A shortage of wind led to an increase in emissions from electricity for the first time in almost 10 years, according to the International Energy Association (IEA). It found that the UK's electricity generated carbon emissions in 2021 were more than a fifth higher than in 2020

The UK has turned to wind energy at the expense of solar power and nuclear. Meanwhile, the National Grid is turning to new forms of battery storage to help spread risk. It is a form of storage that can also be used on housing estates (see below).

Today's houses are mostly not future proof and there is a lot to be done. This includes work on new homes and the legacy housing stock. With 80-85% of today's homes likely still standing in 2050 – and the UK's housing current stock still one of the most inefficient in Europe – greater policy and financial action to drive energy efficiency is essential.

There are two main ways to achieve the necessary reductions in CO2 emissions say WEF. The traditional way is to improve insulation to reduce the amount of heating (or cooling) loss. Think double glazing and roof insulation (both of which lack real housing benefit). An alternative is Passive Housing which is also a powerful tool in this regard. An added innovative, efficient and inexpensive way is to equip buildings with digital tools that allow them to automatically adjust heating, lighting and other systems to the number of people present at any given time, using real-time data analysis. Such "autonomous buildings" can be ultra-efficient, fully electric, perhaps using the emerging light weight solar panels (or vertical windmills) to supply power, which can be managed remotely. Solar water heating systems are now very efficient year round and can even be mounted on a wall.

Meantime, if 80% of new residential buildings in Europe were made of wood, and wood was used in the structures, cladding, surfaces, and furnishings of houses, the buildings would store 55 million tons of carbon dioxide a year. That is equivalent to about 47% of the annual emissions of Europe's cement industry. There are also alternative materials as good or better. One solution is the new alternative to cement now on the near horizon.

Added pressure on the housing sector is driven, and is developing, because of Climate Change, says the Met Office. What is more, the rate of change is faster and accelerating.

The evidence stacks up

Burning hot heat waves, record-breaking storms, threats to water supply and, in turn, damaging and record-breaking floods are well publicised. We have seen wild fires destroying many people's homes, and droughts have become commonplace.

In 2021, September's mean temperature of 14.7°C for the UK was actually quite close to August's figure of 15°C and significantly warmer than average. Father Chrismas is having a hard time. Winter weather is getting too warm for snow. New Year's Day in 2021 and 2022 broke records with temperatures up to 18C. September 2021 was actually only slightly cooler than an average August and was the second warmest on record. The October mean temperature was 10.9 °C, which is 1.4 °C above the 1981-2010 long-term average. By November, the provisional UK mean temperature was 7.0 °C, which is 0.8 °C above the 1981-2010 long-term average (after reaching 40 degrees record in July 2022, they seem quite cool)

However, evidence of mitigation in the building sector does seem to be at the fringes. The need for mitigation is urgent. 'Natural disasters pose a considerable future risk and are occurring much more frequently than mankind has ever known say the Climate Change Committee.

Late in the day, Barrett Homes, the UK's biggest housebuilder, have started work on developing global warming sensitive homes. It is an advanced initiative and worth following. Part of this concept deals with global warming but the impact of Climate Change is muted.

However, it is a long way before it will meet the national need and has to be a worthy exemplar for other builders.

There are added threats from natural disasters to be considered as well.

The Gulf Stream

The Gulf Stream is slowing down. The Met Office describes it thus:

The Gulf Stream is a small part of something called the 'thermohaline circulation or 'Atlantic Meridional Overturning Circulation. This is a large, global-scale ocean conveyor belt driven by differences in temperature and salt content – the water's density.

Originating at the tip of Florida, the Gulf Stream is a warm and swift Atlantic Ocean current that follows the eastern coastline of the US and Canada before crossing the Atlantic Ocean towards Europe. It ensures that the climate of Western Europe is much warmer than it would otherwise be.

In the lifetime of houses built now, we will have to face the effects of the Gulf Stream fading. Stefan Rahmstorf of the Potsdam Institute for Climate Impact Research, who co-authored the study published in Nature Geoscience, told the Guardian that a weakening Gulf Stream would increase the number and severity of storms hitting Britain and will bring more heatwaves to Europe. This is in addition to other current predictions.

He said the circulation had already slowed by about 15%, and the impacts were being seen. "In 20 to 30 years it is likely to weaken further, and that will inevitably influence our weather, so we would see an increase in storms and heatwaves in Europe, (and sea level rises on the east coast of the US)," he said.

CO2 has competition

And then there is Methane. It is much more potent than CO_2 and there is loads of it trapped under ice in the arctic. Atmospheric levels of methane have risen 150% during the past two centuries. By comparison, global CO_2 levels have risen about 50% in the same period. The slope sediments in the Arctic contain a huge quantity of frozen methane and other gases – known as hydrates. Methane has a warming effect 80 times stronger than carbon dioxide over 20 years. The United States Geological Survey has previously listed Arctic hydrate destabilisation as one of four most serious scenarios for abrupt Climate Change.

In 2020, the international team on board the Russian research ship R/V Akademik Keldysh said bubbles were currently dissolving in the water and methane levels at the surface were four to eight times what would normally be expected and this was venting into the atmosphere.

Better detection of where the methane is coming from is becoming a global imperative. An analysis by the International Energy Agency found that methane emissions from oil, gas and coal are about 70% higher than government official reports. If the world is ever going to achieve significant reductions of this gas, it needs to know where it's coming from. New satelites are now reporting where and how much methane is being produced.

All this means that future housing has to recognise the dangers inherent in old and new buildings. Some solutions can be very popular with the electorate and the environmental lobby, others less so. Persuading a wide range of interests that the houses being built and renovated in the 2020s will probably have at least a 30-year life which will be a time when the effects of Climate Change will have a big impact on the population.

We see Climate Change-driven effects everywhere. Progressively they have come closer to home.

As the 26th UN Climate Change Conference of the Parties (COP26) outcomes became apparent, the impact of Climate Change was laid out before us: "The amount by which the previous record has been exceeded should worry us all," said Prof Gabi Hegerl, professor of climate system science at the University of Edinburgh. In some cases, it is a matter of dangerous weather events or drought or, as we are already seeing, deaths caused by heat. It's global and already local in a street near you.

A world of impacts

There are some very compelling global impacts that also need to be explored.

According to the UN, 3.2 billion people live in agricultural areas with high, or very high, water shortages. Of them, 1.2 billion – around one-sixth of the world's population – live in severely water-constrained agricultural areas, mostly in Asia.

Northern Oman was battered by Cyclone Shaheen in 2021, the first tropical cyclone to make it that far west into the Gulf. Around Basra in southern Iraq in 2021, pressure on the grid owing to 50C heat led to constant blackouts, with residents driving around in their air-conditioned cars to stay cool.

Kuwait broke the record for the hottest day ever in 2016 at 53.6, and its 10-day rolling average six years later was equally sweltering. Flash floods occurred in Jeddah, and more recently, Mecca, while across Saudi Arabia, average temperatures have increased by 2%, and the maximum temperatures by 2.5%, all just since the 1980s. To mitigate the Climate Change effect there will be calls on a wide range of resources. People will have to migrate from such effects.

The effect on migration across the world is a matter for consideration, and the consequential effects have to be taken into account over the next few decades. The evidence is compelling. Global warming is contributing to more and extended heat waves, a tripling of droughts, a quadrupling of storms, and a tenfold increase in flooding in Africa since the 1970s — exacerbating security threats on the continent.

In less than 30 years these pressures will cause mass migration, wars, disease and death across the world.

There are other, external, issues.

The horror of the Ukraine war added to the global post-Covid energy inflation with the energy supply to Europe curtailed. In an instant, governments rushed ahead with policies to increase green energy production. More windmill farms, tide race power production and green hydrogen were brought to the fore. The opportunity to disperse generating capacity was ignored. It seems that the bureaucracy does not want lots of little solutions that serve a household or local community (and cost the Treasury nothing). but then there are no longer opportunities for empire building. Big is best. Rooftop solar, vertical windmills on houses. Back-garden solar/hydrogen generators, end of street electricity storage facilities are not even on the bureaucrat's horizon.

Dispersed energy production can be executed very fast. A dozen solar panels on every new house can be implemented in weeks.

The security outlook for the UK and its allies is far more dangerous now than at any time in the past 30 years. The new head of armed forces Admiral Sir Tony Radakin identifies a number of threats.

In 1972, academics at the Massachusetts Institute of Technology (MIT) predicted that our present way of life without regard for environmental and societal costs would lead to society collapsing by the mid 21st century. New research suggests that it could be true.

The Ukraine war is not without its threats to mitigating global warming or Climate Change.

The disruption of the global food supply is now a real concern. With no cereals growing in Ukraine it becomes even more of a desert. A very big dust bowl in the middle of Europe.

We love and hate plastics. But what would happen if an enzyme were to suddenly appear that eats plastics. Not just Coke bottles but washing-up bowls, dresses, umbrellas, loft insulation, gutters and the plastics polluting the seas and all those things we now accept without thinking.

It's behind you... yes, it already exists. Covid is as nothing by comparison. Is our 30 year home plastic enzyme proof?

One wonders if the Royal Institute of British Archtects (RIBA) has commissioned research examining such issues and is advising its architect members on what to do?

Meanwhile, there are other frighteners. We are long overdue for a major volcanic eruption.

The direct migration pressure and more powerful indirect pressure is becoming more obvious and the problem of population growth is but another issue. The world's population is expected to increase by 2 billion persons in the next 30 years, from 7.7 billion currently to 9.7 billion in 2050 according to a new United Nations report. One in five people will be over 65 in 2021 and proportionately getting older all the time. 267 million will be pushed to higher land by rising sea levels and increasing intensity and frequency of extreme weather events, such as abnormally heavy rainfall, prolonged droughts, desertification, environmental degradation, or sea-level rise and cyclones have already caused more than 20 million people to leave their homes and move to other areas in their countries each year says UNHCR.

To what extent will such events affect the need for more or different housing in the UK? We already know that sea level rises will inundate much of our housing stock. The UK's Committee on Climate Change projected that 520,000 properties are already in areas with significant coastal flood risk. However, this may treble to 1.5m by the 2080s without action.

The Ukraine war aside and according to KPMG (Gaya Herrington, the Sustainability and Dynamic System Analysis Lead at KPMG), some events are almost unbelievable. Herrington predicts that humanity's pursuit of economic growth without regard for environmental and social costs would lead to societal collapse by the mid 21st century".

Even narrow economic predictions are fraught and come as science-based Orwellian prognostications. After a remarkable period of stability, stretching from the end of World War II to the early 21st century is coming to an end. A huge economy has all but collapsed as a consequence of the Russian invasion of the Ukraine. The economic and political pressures emerging in Russia do not bode well for global warming mitigation and re-homing 10 million refugees across Europe will put pressure on moves towards building and upgrading homes in a warming world.

The Met Office has even modelled civil collapse in its work on Climate Change.

In the UK, the demands on government and, especially the Treasury and local government post-Covid, are tough. The black storms created by Russia are worse.

How societies organise themselves to respond to cascading impacts exacerbated by Climate Change will help define the future of disaster planning, mitigation, response, and recovery. Current emergency management risk analyses focus on identifying a broad array of threats and hazards that may affect an area.

However, there is limited attention and understanding of the totality of hazard impacts. The dangers of not having critical capabilities to rapidly manage impact (including the potential of new incidents within incidents e.g. disease following floods) is urgent. In building, upgrading and repurposing houses, the potential for significant disruption has to be part of the planning process. It is not unreasonable to think of storms causing flooding in Leadhills, the highest village in the UK. Nowhere is exempt. Every development has to be designed for such disasters at ever more frequent intervals.

There are management techniques that include artificial intelligence and issues and crisis management is nowhere near as hard as many would imagine. These considerations have to be part of the developer's and housing refurbishing plans and not just the responsibility of local authorities. After all, it is the developer that is seeking permission and presenting a case for development. One would recommend reading the briefing on how housing has been assessed in the latest UK Climate Change Risk Assessment (CCRA) Technical Report.

The whole building sector has to step up to the mark, says the Centre for Sustainable Energy.

The Impacts - a liturgy

Policymakers at every level need to consider the effects of Climate Change on their sphere of activity.

The Imperial College papers are useful to inform thinking as its academics' view the effects of Climate Change and Energy.

Global temperatures will continue to rise for decades to come.

The Intergovernmental Panel on Climate Change forecasts a temperature rise of 2.5 to 10 degrees Fahrenheit over the next century. This means there is a need for homes that can cope with such extremes.

Because human-induced warming is superimposed on a naturally varying climate, the temperature rise has not been, and will not be, uniform or smooth across all countries or over time. Without aggressive global climate action, experts fear heat waves could reach 48 degrees Celsius (a searing

118 degrees Fahrenheit) in London by late this century. That is, during the lifetime of our grandchildren.

The reality of Climate Change was evident in September 2021. A major storm in Spain caused flash flooding in Alacnar, which quickly turned into rivers that swept away everything in their path. Around a dozen cars ended up tossed in the surf of the Mediterranean Sea. The flooding was also evident as far away as Madrid. North Korea's state news agency reported that heavy rains in the northeast destroyed and flooded more than a thousand homes.

This happened during the week the Ida storm turned New York subways into storm sewers, and major highways became house destroying torrents. In Louisiana, a million homes were without power. In the same week, massive drought enhanced fires blackened skies in California and the Amazon rainforest. Extreme weather and deadly flooding in Germany were evident, and wildfires were rapidly destroying parts of Greece and Turkey. In the US, Australia and Canada wildfires wiped out entire towns and villages in the same week in 2021.

But it can't happen here.

Climate Change is already being felt across the UK. All of the top-ten warmest years for the UK in records back to 1884 have occurred since 2002, and, for central England, the 21st century so far has been warmer than the previous three centuries. The extremes are already with us and more often.

The UK record of 38.7C in 2021 is a bit worrying already based on current research:

"Our survey of the climate record from station data reveals many global temperature exceedances of 31° and 33°C and two stations that have already reported multiple daily maximum values above 35°C. Essentially we are getting close to annual temperatures that kill people. Then there was the shock. In July 2022 the new record was over 40 degrees.

Homes need to be built and refurbished to mitigate effects of heat waves and storms. This is not just a question of house insulation to reduce global warming there are other considerations needed to protect us from Climate Change. Cars washed away in a storm is a disruptive circumstance for all concerned. House and estate design can reduce such domestic disasters and so they should.

Storms Ciara and Dennis, hitting the UK only one week apart, were part of the UK's wettest February on record and brought devastating flooding affecting many homes and businesses. It was also a dry and exceptionally sunny spring in 2020, especially across the southern half of the UK, with over 150% of average sunshine across England and Wales.

Other notable weather extremes from 2020 include eight further named storms (in addition to Ciara and Dennis). More climate developments included a record of 37.8°C at Heathrow on 3 July 2021 with extreme rainfall in Norfolk. Not forgetting the 40.3-degree record in 2022.

A study published in the journal Nature Climate Change finds that winds across much of North America, Europe and Asia have been growing faster since about 2010. In less than a decade, the global average wind speed has increased from about 7 mph to about 7.4 mph. For the average wind turbine, that translates to a 17% increase in potential wind energy.

The tales continue: The electricity provider Northern Powergrid, said 16,000 customers were without power as of Wednesday, December 1 2021. After 3 days of disruption caused by high winds and blizzard conditions, the electricity distributor had restored power to 224,000 of the 240,000 homes and businesses impacted by the storm. But, tens of thousands faced no power for over two weeks. A 60 year event. Our houses can, and now have to be, built and renovated to mitigate such disasters. Especially as the following storm Bara (three weeks later) delivered rain, snow, floods and 86 mph winds.

There is an imperative to change housing

Rising sea levels, shrinking ice caps, harsher heatwaves, dangerous precipitation, winds each month breaking records and generally more erratic weather, have catastrophic effects on our environment.

These problems affect power, gas, roads, buildings, bridges and railways and most other aspects of infrastructure. In addition, there are threats to biodiversity and natural habitats. Sea levels are rising. Severe storms can dump huge amounts of water in anyone's street.

The major impacts of sea-level rise occur during high tides and storms, causing flooding along coastlines and estuaries. In 2018 the Climate Change Committee (CCC), the Government's independent advisers on Climate Change, said that by the 2080s (just 60 years from now) in England, "up to 1.5 million properties, including 1.2 million homes, maybe in areas at a significant level of [coastal] flood risk".

Annual damages cost from flooding alone could increase to between £2bn and £12bn by the 2080s. Houses now need to be away from such risks or mitigation has to be, and in a number of cases has been, implemented regularly.

The UK could also face threats to its water security and supply. Declining summer river flows, reduced groundwater replenishment, and increased evaporation could contribute to water loss, water shortages and restrictions on usage according to the Environment Agency. The question having been raised, are there solutions available to the building sector? Yes there are. The big issue is whether builders and restorers in the housing sector can bite the bullet and add storage mitigation add-ons to the traditional home. Harvesting, storing and cleaning water is possible even on a domestic scale and certainly for a highrise block of flats. A telling sign of a poorly thought through estate design is the size of the gutters. The tiny ones are certainly not capable of managing a Climate Change storm.

The significance of extreme events like floods and heatwaves is important, but there is an accompanying concern for planners. The nature of our current environment effect is inconvenient for most, awful for some people and points to a much more cataclysmic future. Additionally, climate scientists have long emphasised the importance of climate tipping points like thawing permafrost, ice sheet disintegration, and changes in atmospheric and ocean circulation.

The reality is that such events can suddenly change the dynamics of the world's climate. It is for governments to model such emergencies but in their crisis planning, they will have to take the building sector into their plans.

When Covid19 lockdowns stopped air traffic, the impact of less CO_2 on Climate Change and noise pollution was evident for all to see.

Planning for technologies that spring on us and are out of control can be different to Covid. Imagine what happens when an experimental bug escapes a laboratory releasing a polythene eating global virus! Government crisis 'war games' now have to consider the climate when planning ameliorating solutions. Houses too need to have some in-built protection as a matter of course.

Global warming is life-changing and will change where we live dramatically. It is possible to go forward or we will go backwards.

Sources and Reference Works Cited

Centre for Sustainable Energy: Welcome, https://www.cse.org.uk/. Accessed 25 March 2022.

"Barratt Developments launches the Z House: a flagship zero carbon concept home." Barratt Developments Plc, 25 October 2021, https://www.barrattdevelopments.co.uk/media/media releases/pr-2 021/pr-25-10-2021. Accessed 12 March 2022.

Borunda, Alejandra. "Heat waves kill people—and Climate Change is making it much, much worse." National Geographic, 2 July 2021, https://www.nationalgeographic.com/environment/article/heat-relat ed-deaths-attributed-to-climate-change. Accessed 25 March 2022.

"Bugs Are Evolving to Eat Plastic, Study Finds." Yale E360, 22 December 2021,https://e360.yale.edu/digest/bugs-are-evolving-to-eat-plastic-study- finds. Accessed 13 March 2022.

"Buildings are the foundation of our energy-efficient future." The World Economic Forum, 22 February 2021, https://www.weforum.org/agenda/2021/02/why-the-buildings-of-th e-future-are-key-to-an-efficient-energy-ecosystem/. Accessed 12 March 2022.

"Carbon Literacy Guide - UK Health Alliance." The UK Health Alliance on Climate Change, December2021, http://www.ukhealthalliance.org/carbon-literacy-guide/#science. Accessed 12 March 2022.

Carey, Bjorn. "Stanford scientists: Climate Change on pace to occur 10 times faster than any change recorded in past 65 million years." Stanford News, 1 August 2013, https://news.stanford.edu/news/2013/august/Climate Change-speed- 080113.html. Accessed 12 March 2022.

"Climate Change continues to be evident across UK." Met Office, 29July2021, https://www.metoffice.gov.uk/about-us/press-office/news/weather- and-climate/2021/climate-change-continues-to-be-evident-across-uk. Accessed 25 March 2022.

"Energy and climate | Faculty of Natural Sciences." Imperial College London, https://www.imperial.ac.uk/environmental-policy/research/themes/ energy-climate/. Accessed 25 March 2022.

"Energy Performance of Building Certificates in England and Wales: October to December 2021." GOV.UK, https://www.gov.uk/government/statistics/energy-performance-of-b uilding-certificates-in-england-and-wales-october-to-december-20

21. Accessed 12 March 2022.

"Energy Storage to Support the UK Transmission Grid." Form Energy, 27 October 2021, https://formenergy.com/insights/energy-storage-to-support-the-uk-t ransmission-grid/. Accessed 12 March 2022.

"Environment | Us/environment." The Guardian, 25 February 2021, https://www.theguardian.com/environment/2021/feb/25. Accessed 7 March 2022.

"expert reaction to the 31st State of the Climate report." Science Media Centre, 25 August 2021, https://www.sciencemediacentre.org/expert-reaction-to-the-31st-sta te-of-the-climate-repo rt/. Accessed 25 March 2022.

"Exploring Passive House Design - 90% Energy Savings!" YouTube, 23 February 2021, https://www.youtube.com/watch?v=secB3R0sIYU. Accessed   12 March 2022.

Garrood, Michael. "Dust storms, dry rivers, and desertification in Ukraine offer harsh lessons against intensive farming." Euromaidan Press, 6 May 2020, https://euromaidanpress.com/2020/05/06/ecology-environment-dus t-storms-dry-rivers-an d-desertification-in-ukraine-offer-harsh-lessons-against-intensive-f arming-climate-change s/. Accessed 13 March 2022.

"Greener AND cheaper: Graphene@Manchester solves concrete's big problem." The University of Manchester, 25 May 2021,

https://www.manchester.ac.uk/discover/news/greener-and-cheaper- graphenemanchester-solves-concretes-big-problem/. Accessed 28

March 2022.

Harvey, Fiona. "Atlantic Ocean circulation at weakest in a millennium, say scientists." The Guardian, 25 February 2021,

https://www.theguardian.com/environment/2021/feb/25/atl antic-oc ean-circulation-at-weakest-in-a-millennium-say-scientists. Accessed 25 March 2022.

"Heatwave will create a hidden natural disaster in the UK this weekend - Grantham Research

Institute on Climate Change and the environment." London School of Economics, 16 July 2021,

https://www.lse.ac.uk/granthaminstitute/news/heatwave-will-createidden-natural-disaster-in-the-uk-this-weekend/.Accessed   25 March 2022.

"How satellites may hold the key to the methane crisis." The Guardian, 7 March 2022, https://www.theguardian.com/environment/2022/mar/06/how-satell ites-may-hold-the-key-to-the-methane-crisis. Accessed 13 March 2022.

"Hydrogen breakthrough at Unilever factory." Liverpool Business News, 9 March 2022, https://lbndaily.co.uk/hydrogen-breakthrough-at-unilever-factory/. Accessed 13 March 2022.

"Iceland volcano: why we were lucky we weren't wiped out." The Guardian, 21 April 2010, https://www.theguardian.com/world/2010/apr/21/iceland-volcano-a sh-extinction-human-r ace. Accessed 13 March 2022.

"KU Leuven team creates solar panel that produces hydrogen from moisture in air." Green Car Congress, 8 March 2019, https://www.greencarcongress.com/2019/03/20190308-kul.html. Accessed 13 March 2022.

Liberatore, Stacy. "MIT's 1972 prediction of the collapse of society is on track to happen by 2040, study reveals." Daily Mail, 14 July 2021, https://www.dailymail.co.uk/sciencetech/article-9788957/MITs-19 72-prediction-collapse-society-track-happen-2040-study-reveals.ht ml. Accessed 13 March 2022.

"Limits to Growth." KPMG Advisory Services,
https://advisory.kpmg.us/articles/2021/limits-to-
growth.html.

Accessed 25 March 2022.

Lotze, Hermann. "New IPCC report on climate impacts."
Potsdam Institute for Climate Impact Research, 28
February 2022,

https://www.pik-potsdam.de/en/news/latest-news/pik-lead-
authors- on-ipcc-report-on-climate-impacts. Accessed 4
March 2022.

McGrath, Matt. "climate change: Europe's 2020 heat
reached 'troubling'   level." BBC, 25   August 2021,
https://www.bbc.co.uk/news/science-environment-
58333124. Accessed 4 March 2022.

"Migration and global environmental change: future
challenges and opportunities."GOV.UK,
https://assets.publishing.service.gov.uk/government/upload
s/syste m/uploads/attachment

_data/file/287717/11-1116-migration-and-global-
environmental-ch ange.pdf. Accessed 7 March 2022.

"More than 12 million UK people face severe health risks
or death from climate crisis, study says." The Independent,
5 February 2021,

https://www.independent.co.uk/climate-change/news/uk-deaths-he atwaves-flooding-health-b1798065.html. Accessed 4 March 2022.

Mulhern, Owen. "Too Hot To Live: Climate Change In Saudi Arabia." Earth.Org, 30 October 2020, https://earth.org/data_visualization/intolerable-saudi-summers-to-b ecome-much-longer-b y-2070/. Accessed 25 March 2022.

"Nature has learnt how to eat our plastic!" YouTube, 31 May 2020,

https://www.youtube.com/watch?v=rtZs-MPFcHo. Accessed 7 March 2022.

Nebo, B. "GLOBAL WARMING AND AFRICA." Global Human

Tragedy, 15 November 2021, https://globalhumantragedy.co.uk/global-warming-and-africa/. Accessed 25 March 2022.

Ogasa, Nikk. "A UN report shows Climate Change's escalating toll on people and nature." Science News, 28 February 2022,

https://www.sciencenews.org/article/climate-united-nations-ipcc-re port-people-nature. Accessed 25 March 2022.

"Our homes are not ready for Climate Change." Local Government Association, https://www.local.gov.uk/our-homes-are-not-ready climate-change. Accessed 12 March 2022.

Owen, Glenn. "Met Office predicts the collapse of society following climate disaster." Daily Mail, 15 January 2022, https://www.dailymail.co.uk/news/article-10406521/Met-Office-pr edicts-collapse-society-following-climate-disaster.html. Accessed 7 March 2022.

Owen, Glenn. "Met Office predicts the collapse of society following climate disaster." Daily Mail, 15 January 2022, https://www.dailymail.co.uk/news/article-10406521/Met-Office-pr edicts-collapse-society-following-climate-disaster.html. Accessed 13 March 2022.

Polityuk, Pavel, et al. "Ukraine to support crop sowing campaign, says prime minister." Reuters, 13 March 2022, https://www.reuters.com/world/europe/ukraine-support-crop-sowin g-campaign-says-prime-minister-2022-03-13/. Accessed 13 March 2022.

Rigby, Sara. "Super-enzyme breaks down plastic bottles in 'a matter of days.'" BBC Science Focus Magazine, 29 September 2020, https://www.sciencefocus.com/news/super-enzyme-breaks-down-p lastic-bottles-in-a-matter-of-days/. Accessed 25 March 2022.

"Summer heatwaves killed 900 people across UK, official data indicates | The Independent." The Independent, 7 January 2020,

https://www.independent.co.uk/news/uk/home-news/summer-heat waves-uk-deaths-weather-climate-change-phe-a9273546.html. Accessed 13 March 2022.

"Technical Report." UK Climate Risk,

https://www.ukclimaterisk.org/independent-assessment ccra3/tech nical-report/. Accessed 25 March 2022.

"UK struggling to keep pace with Climate Change impacts." Climate Change Committee, 16 June 2021, https://www.theccc.org.uk/2021/06/16/uk-struggling-to-keep-pace- with-climate-change-impacts/. Accessed 25 March 2022.

Voegele, Juergen. "Millions on the move: What Climate Change could mean for internal migration." World Bank Blogs, 1 November 2021, https://blogs.worldbank.org/voices/millions-move-what-climate-ch ange-could-mean-internal-migration. Accessed 25 March 2022.

Watts, Jonathan. "Arctic methane deposits 'starting to release', scientists say." The Guardian, 27 October 2020,

https://www.theguardian.com/science/2020/oct/27/sleeping
-giant-a rctic-methane-deposits-starting-to-release-
scientists-find. Accessed 25 March 2022.

"What is the Gulf Stream?" Met Office,
https://www.metoffice.gov.uk/weather/learn-
about/weather/oceans/

what-is-the-gulf-stream. Accessed 25 March 2022.

Chapter 3: The Housing Stock

There is a housing crisis.

But what do we mean by 'housing'? What is the stock of housing in the UK, and how close is it to meeting population needs?

There is an almost hidden part of the 'housing stock'. It is the underused and decaying portion, much-hated by the population at large according to YouGov polls. It is dealt with here as well.

In 2021 the Guardian pointed out that House prices appear to have defied economic gravity over the past year. The lockdowns triggered by the pandemic led to a 10% fall in GDP, the largest fall in 300 years since the Great Frost of 1709. Yet the latest data show house prices have grown at the fastest annual rate – 13.4% – in 17 years. Are we in the midst of another housing bubble?

One might add 'or is this a market response reflecting the dearth of houses'. So, how many houses are there?

How many homes?

To house 67 million people, there were 24.7 million dwellings in March 2022, but 0.9% were empty.

Some are plain grotty. Many are just too expensive to live in. Many leasehold flats have maintenance charges of £1,200 a year - more than double in 2007.

As of 2019, more than 3.12 million owner-occupied houses were built before 1919. By contrast, approximately 1.5 million owner-occupied dwellings were produced from 2003 onwards.

Furthermore, the number of owner-occupied houses under construction has decreased through the years. Even with the loss of buildings over time, most owner-occupied dwellings in England were constructed in 1980 or before. In 2019, there were around 15 million owner-occupied households in England.

In 2021, the Bank of England (BoE) chief economist Andy Haldane said: "...the housing market in the UK is on fire", a fact plain for all to see. The leading house price indices (Halifax and Nationwide) show year-on-year increases exceeding 10 per cent.

Starting in 2022, tens of thousands of homes will be built on derelict sites as part of a year of new urban housing. In urban areas, house building is very smart, and has enough shrubs and trees to make Robin Hood proud but they are built speculatively and not to satisfy local needs. This is an urban housing subsidy paid to meet regional cities' needs. We are subsidising the speculator's guesswork.

The Chancellor also announced a fund to transform previously developed land equivalent to 2,000 football pitches in 2021.

It's all a mismatch of policy mumbo jumbo added to Bla Bla Bla with a dash of Downing Street spokesperson business meetings.

The housing stock in England, in March 2019, had 26.7 million dwellings.

- 15.6 million owner-occupied,

- 7 million private rented,

- 2.5 million rented from private registered providers (housing associations)

- 1.6 million rented from local authorities.

- In 2013, buy-to-rent investors — referred to as buy-to-let (BTL) in the United Kingdom — accounted for 13% of all UK mortgage-funded housing transactions and an even more significant fraction of non-mortgage sales.

The government says that the number of new homes needed in England is 345,000 per year.

The House of Lords Select Committee on Economic Affairs concluded in its report 'Building More Homes' (2016), that the present house building target "was not based on a robust analysis" and went on to recommend that the housing crisis required the development of at least 300,000 new homes annually "for the foreseeable future." In addition to questioning whether a target of over 300,000 homes is ambitious enough, there was some doubt over whether the number was achievable.

The building statistics are a bit confusing.

In 2019/20, the total housing stock in England increased by around 244,000 homes. This is about 1% higher than the year before but is still lower than the estimated need.

Housing need manifests itself in a variety of ways, such as in solving increased levels of overcrowding, acute affordability issues, young people living with their parents for more extended periods, and impaired labour mobility (resulting in businesses finding it difficult to recruit and retain staff), and increased levels of homelessness. Then there is the problem of "fit for Climate Change dwellings", which is the majority of all homes.

Older properties need to be updated. Around 18% of the UK's annual CO_2 emissions come from existing homes, which will still be standing in 2050. 80% of 2050's homes have already been built. It is also widely acknowledged that the retrofit challenge is monumental. Every year over one million homes will need to be retrofitted for 30 years. We cannot afford to retrofit them twice.

But if we retrofit them well, we can enjoy many environmental, social and economic benefits.

New houses need help to achieve sales. 313,043 households have now bought a home with the support of the Government's 'Help to Buy' Equity Loan Scheme. The question to ask is whether the houses were built to meet the local need or were they built speculatively and required subsidies to sell them?

House price escalation has attracted fund investment resulting in circular property inflation. Meantime the housing stock cannot match the needs of a growing population (this applies in Scotland and Wales as well).

As the government White Paper puts it: "It is no longer unusual for houses to "earn" more than the people living in them. In 2015, the average home in the South East of England increased in value by £29,000, while the average annual pay in the region was just £24,542. The average London home made its owner more than £22 an hour during the working week in 2015 considerably more than the average Londoner's hourly rate. That's good news if you own a property in the capital, but it's a big barrier to entry if you don't.

Many houses are in poor condition, and a significant proportion of the housing stock is unused.

	2011 Census (Thousands)	% of all households	% change 2001-2011
All households without dependent children	16,575	70.9	8.5
One person households	7,067	30.2	8.7
One-family households	8,270	35.4	5.9
No children	6,022	25.8	4.2
Non-dependent children	2,248	9.6	10.7
Other	1,238	5.3	29.2

Source: 2001 and 2011 Census, Office for National Statistics

There were 225,845 Long-Term Vacant Dwellings in England in 2019, an increase of 9,659 (4.5%) from 216,186 in 2018. Long-term vacant dwellings at 0.9 per cent of the 2019 dwelling stock in England are an interesting underutilised housing asset.

Thus we have knowledge of the nature of the housing stock in the UK. There would seem to be a lot to be done not only to add to the housing stock but to bring the existing properties to be Climate Change ready.

At one end of the market are houses built by speculators. We see them in monstrous housing estates tacked onto small towns and villages across the country. But what we tend not to see are the unoccupied houses hidden in slums and lone dwellings like rotting teeth tucked away in long streets of late 19th and early 20th-century housing speculation. A third of the mansions on the most expensive stretch of London's Bishops Avenue are standing empty, including several huge houses that have fallen into ruin after standing almost completely vacant for a quarter of a century.

The data do not show the number of multiple-family households that are hidden in 5.3% of 'Other' dwellings which is growing very fast.

There is another significant number which is the number of Non-dependant children staying with mum and dad. Is this a reflection of not being able to rent or buy as an alternative to staying at home?

Empty Houses

This is largely a part of the Housing Stock that is not really part of the range of dwellings in use and so is considered in some depth here.

In 2017 there was a year-on-year rise of 42,540 to a total of 268,385 long-term empty homes in England. This was the fourth consecutive year in which figures had risen. It's a rise of almost 20% which meant that the national total had increased by over a third (34%) since 2016. Even today, this trend continues and continues to accelerate.

'Action on Empty Homes' reports that besides London: "...Other cities facing housing pressures see similar big rises which the (COVID) pandemic may be exacerbating - Manchester saw an annual rise of 19% to 1,455. Birmingham is up 18% to 5,386 long-term empty homes. Liverpool is up 17% to 4,631.

Areas in the North, where communities are blighted by under-investment and empty homes, have remained stubbornly high in recent years. Bradford now has a staggering 4,091 long-term empty homes (nearly 1 in every 50). Hartlepool has over 1,000 after a massive 36% increase in 2020 alone. Middlesborough also saw a massive 29% increase to over 1,500 long-term empty homes, and Grimsby and North East Lincolnshire have 1,636 long-term empty homes (1 in every 45 homes).

Such numbers can be juxtaposed with the 96,600 households in temporary accommodation at the end of June 2021 (which excludes those hidden away in public, private and domestic social care). Much of the costs are a further drain on the public purse but are largely hidden by the maze of national and local government departments involved.

The buildings involved are mostly, but by no means all, in modern day slums.

Empty dwellings vary from abandoned house to completely derelict buildings and of course, not all of them are safe to be lived in or even economically viable to be renovated into liveable properties. Some of these buildings are owner-occupied, and some have shared ownership. Many are rented or are in the hands of landlords operating in a grey economy and on the edge of the law (including those who use the properties to temporarily 'house' the disadvantaged, including immigrants and the homeless).

There are buildings and there is a market for solving this sector of the housing asset.

The cost, of course, falls on taxpayers including ratepayers, VAT payers, NI payers, Car Park payers and all the other jumble of methods to finance this sector of the economy. These poor housing conditions have an additional cost. The health of the residents.

Analysis by the Building Research Establishment shows the annual costs to the NHS of poor quality and hazardous housing at £1.4 billion. This rises to £18.5 billion p.a. when more total societal costs are included (long term care, mental health etc.).

Temporary accommodation spending has grown to £1.2bn with the majority being paid to private companies by government agencies.

All this money is made available year on year. By diverting it into reviving and repurposing houses and providing homes, jobs are created. Thus costs are turned into assets, and deprivation is turned into excellent long term homes.

Back of the envelope calculations show that £10,000,000 of public money could be redirected or saved by updating unoccupied dwellings. Yes, Chancellor, no hike in spending or taxes, just better government and then the poorest of households can each have a Passive House palace to live in (but imagine the tussle there would be in attempting to wrestle £1.4 billion from the NHS to improve the health of people living in near derelict properties!).

It's not going to be an instant magic cure. Still, there are opportunities to apply significantly more powerful pressure on the political, government and administrative institutions to get the job done.

There are other hidden benefits that can be exemplified by examining the reduction of doctors and nurses needed to care for fewer 'poor housing' patients. Smaller government is possible by 'Levelling Up' the quality of the housing stock (see below).

Achieving such a dramatic change and replacing these dwellings with a 30-year Climate Change (Passive Housing +) mitigated alternative will require a political push of immense proportions. It would seem to be a role for a tough Secretary of State for Levelling Up, Housing and Communities.

Moving on from those dwellings that are not in use we can look at a range of dwelling types in subsequent chapters and how these parts of the housing stock can be built, modernised, and re-purposed. A large part of this centres on the financial aspects of the housing stock and re-educated and trained people and is dealt with in the chapter on finance.

An excellent range of dwellings is considered in this book, and there are exciting aspects to the housing stock. In addition to repurposing 'empty' properties, this book needs to look at tower blocks, converted offices, warehouses and other repurposed buildings, multi-story dwellings, low rise, Detached/semi and terraced houses, back-to-back and single storey homes.

Now we are looking at reviving, repurposing, and new builds that offer an opportunity to create beautiful homes that meet housing needs, mitigate the causes of Climate Change and protect from the causes of Global Warming. We may also be on the way to finding money to do all this.

Sources and Reference Works Cited

https://link.springer.com/article/10.1007/s00382-020-05583-x.

The UK Health Alliance on Climate Change, 6 September 2021,http://www.ukhealthalliance.org/. Accessed 2 March 2022.

"Buildings are the foundation of our energy-efficient future." The World Economic Forum, 22 February 2021, https://www.weforum.org/agenda/2021/02/why-the-buildings-of-th e-future-are-key-to-an-efficient-energy-ecosystem/. Accessed 2 March 2022.

"Carbon Literacy Guide - UK Health Alliance." The UK Health Alliance on Climate Change, 6 December 2021, http://www.ukhealthalliance.org/carbon-literacy-guide/#science. Accessed 2 March 2022.

"Energy Performance of Building Certificates in England and Wales: October to December 2021." GOV.UK, https://www.gov.uk/government/statistics/energy-performance-of-b uilding-certificates-in-england-and-wales-october-to-december-20

21. Accessed 2 March 2022.

"Energy Performance of Building Certificates in England and Wales: October to December 2021." GOV.UK, https://www.gov.uk/government/statistics/energy-performance-of-b uilding-certificates-in-england-and-wales-october-to-december-2021. Accessed 2 March 2022.

"Existing and future technologies for retrofitting the UK housing stock – CREDS." CREDS, 8 June 2021, https://www.creds.ac.uk/publications/existing-and-future-technolo gies-for-retrofitting-the-uk-housing-stock/. Accessed 2 March 2022.

"Flood-prone houses may have to be sacrificed, says Environment Agency." The Times, 3 January 2022, https://www.thetimes.co.uk/article/flood-prone-houses-may-have-t o-be-sacrificed-says-environment-agency-qf582lfwr. Accessed 2 March 2022.

"Free Leftover Building Materials Marketplace." Enviromate, 12 July 2016, https://www.enviromate.co.uk/blog/eleven-green-building-material s-way-better-concrete. Accessed 2 March 2022.

"Future Fens flood risk management." GOV.UK, 11 May 2021, https://www.gov.uk/government/news/future-fens-flood-risk-mana gement. Accessed 2 March 2022.

Harvey, Fiona. "World's climate scientists to issue stark warning over global heating threat." The Guardian, 8 August 2021, https://www.theguardian.com/environment/2021/aug/08/worlds-cli mate-scientists-to-issue-stark-warning-over-global-heating-threat. Accessed 2 March 2022.

"Humans 'using one and a half planets' worth of resources and will need two Earths by 2030." Daily Mail, 14 October 2010, https://www.dailymail.co.uk/sciencetech/article-1320419/Humans- using-half-planets-worth-resources-need-Earths-2030.html. Accessed 2 March 2022.

"Mimicking mother nature: Algae-inspired technology makes fresh water." The Brighter Side of News, 22 February 2022, https://www.thebrighterside.news/post/mimicking-mother-nature-a lgae-inspired-technology-makes-fresh-water. Accessed 2 March 2022.

"Novel photocatalyst effectively turns carbon dioxide into methane fuel with light." City University of Hong Kong, 28 January 2021, https://www.cityu.edu.hk/research/stories/2021/01/28/novel -photoc atalyst-effectively-turns-carbon-dioxide-methane-fuel-light. Accessed 2 March 2022.

"Our homes are not ready for Climate Change." Local Government Association, https://www.local.gov.uk/our-homes-are-not-ready-climate-change. Accessed 2 March 2022.

Parr, Doug. "Analysis: Half of UK's electricity to be renewable by 2025." Carbon Brief, 12 April 2019, https://www.carbonbrief.org/analysis-half-uks-electricity-to-be-ren ewable-by-2025. Accessed 2 March 2022.

"Passive House Institute." Passivhaus Institut, https://passivehouse.com/03_certification/02_certification_ buildin gs/06_process/06_process.html. Accessed 2 March 2022.

Ro, Christine. "The 'green' row over the UK's largest renewable power plant." BBC, 14 January 2022, https://www.bbc.co.uk/news/business-59546281. Accessed 2 March 2022.

"UK Climate Change Risk Assessment 2022." GOV.UK, 17 January 2022, https://www.gov.uk/government/publications/uk-climate-change-ri sk-assessment-2022. Accessed 2 March 2022.

"UK housing: Fit for the future?" Climate Change Committee, 21 February 2019, https://www.theccc.org.uk/publication/uk-housing-fit-for-the-futur e/. Accessed 2 March 2022.

"UK housing: Fit for the future?" Climate Change Committee, 21 February 2019, https://www.theccc.org.uk/publication/uk-housing-fit-for-the-futur e/. Accessed 2 March 2022.

Chapter 4: The 30 Year House

A large proportion of our existing homes in the UK are over 50 years old. It follows that modernising and building new homes will require the relevant professions to look into the future.

What will a house look like in 2050?

We have to peer into the future and hope that we are right. What is certain from the COP26 conference (26th UN Climate Change Conference of the Parties (COP26) Glasgow 2021) is that small steps spell doom.

Go into a modern housing estate. Look up. Are the gutters big? If not, they are not ready for the record breaking tempests Climate Change will deliver this year and next. The architect who designs such fixtures should be banned from the Royal Society. Or, perhaps the Royal Institution of Chartered Architects (RICA) should relinquish its Charter status so its members can create rubbish houses without embarrassing the Queen. It is now time to create and build for the future and well beyond the minimum standards introduced by the hosts of COP26, the British Government.

Let's be certain about this. Restoring, insuring and living in dwellings that are not Climate Change mitigated is far more expensive than renovating, refurbishing and re-building poorly prepared homes.

It is easy to kick the Climate Change can down the road but evidence of how it can affect us NOW is frightening but there are some drivers lining up.

The main cause of the 2022 gas price crisis has grown because of the increasing gas demand (organically, following the pandemic) and reduced gas supplies caused by the Ukraine war. Additionally, unseasonably low wind generation in the UK (particularly in September 2021 and the winter of 2022) reduced green energy availability.

Lower pipeline gas flows from Russia to Europe (and other Europeans have similar housing problems and bigger gas supply issues). Less storage capacity, and higher carbon prices have focused minds on developing carbon-reduced power. It is a narrow perspective. There is a need for a much wider view of these issues.

The home of the future will need long-term policies to keep the lights on.

Will government encourage the use of new materials and communication without wires, wifi or Bluetooth that are already appearing on the market?

Will roofs protect against heat waves without using mains power to maintain a healthy population?

In June 2022, the government introduced a new set of regulations for new house builders. They set new standards for ventilation, energy efficiency and heating, and state that new residential buildings must have charging points for electric vehicles.

The Federation of Master Builders says the measures will require new materials, testing methods, products and systems to be installed. Indeed so it will. The price of Climate Change mitigation is not cheap.

There are new government rules concerning the amount of glazing used in extensions, and any new windows or doors must be highly insulated." The problem is that the rules will aim to reduce the size of windows that are potentially a source of a lot of solar power.

Some say that walls will have to be thicker in order to comply with requirements for better insulation. Alternatively, new materials may make them thinner but the building sector has not got there yet.

Glazing on windows, doors and roof lights must cover no more than 25% of the floor area to prevent heat loss according to the new regulations which is a rule that has already been superseded

As properties become more airtight, the regulator says there have to be measures to ensure proper airflow, such as having small openings (trickle vents) on windows that allow ventilation when a window is closed. Tosh! Do the job properly, save the NHS billions with proper air filtration.

For people extending their homes, they may be required to install a new, or replacement, heating system depending on the size of the build and have to use lower temperature water to deliver the same heat, which will require increased insulation of pipes commented an insider. It's a big rock for all these 'experts' to hide under. Solar water heating is getting really good. Why not use it?

So the government get 5 out of ten for initiative and 2 out of ten for understanding what is needed and possible. It can also be said that technologies are moving so fast that some of these government initiatives are passed, before the ink has dried on their parchment.

Meantime we also have to consider the prospect of poor quality housing in a time of fast-expanding populations and accelerating environmental change will be dangerous but also a magnet for disruption by the green-eyed disadvantaged.

In the foreseeable (next 30 years), houses will need to be easily maintained and repurposed in part or whole as technologies emerge. The need and cost of structural maintenance also have to be reduced.

Below is a whole chapter on finance. We have to examine how homes will be financed. There will be new forms of finance emerging to unstitch the excesses of builder speculation going back a couple of centuries.

It is not possible to think of a future house in the image of a house being built in 2022 and its close cousin that was built to house 18th-century coal miners.

Let's start with something simple. The northern latitude house does not need to use the power grid, summer or winter (this capability already exists) and using solar power is National Grid energy independent.

In early 2022 there was a proposal for a new £600m solar farm in Cambridgeshire. The scheme would provide power for up to 100,000 homes and will cover nearly 2,800 acres which is 10 times bigger than any other land-based scheme in Britain. It is one of more than 900 solar farms in the planning pipeline to help provide green energy.

There are a number of problems with this approach. The frst is that it is a proposal for another single power plant. This will depend on National Grid power lines to distribute the power despite the prospect of big storms tearing down the infrastructure and consequential power cuts. With a centre this size its ability to provide constant energy when the sun does not shine will be another case of intermittent power requiring big centralised batteries. It is a potential blight in the countryside eight times bigger than Hyde Park in central London. Additionally, the whole process of planning, construction, cabling and commissioning will take a long time. At a time when there is a need for more energy because of added demand set against the restrictions resulting from Covid and the Ukrainian war, long-time coming vulnerable centralised power plants just don't make sense. The alternative dispersed, fast-implemented, mesh power and storage capability proposed in this book will be more reliable even in the worst climate-driven disasters (not to mention war and riot). Big vulnerable systems make little sense, take time to implement, when there are alternatives that cost the exchequer nothing. There is an experiment in Swindon to install a city-wide battery storage capability. It is too big and too vulnerable. Your average yob could switch of all the lights in town with a well-aimed crowbar.

The alternative is so easy as a response to the needs created by the Ukrainian crisis. If every new house were to include 12/24KW or more solar energy (and or other power sources such as vertical wind power), it would represent enough additional electricity for 300,000 houses per year.

The domestic resource would also provide a free alternative power source for transport such as EV, hydrogen of other power-source cars.

There already is a vast range of power storage systems from tiny home batteries to town back-up systems that are green, simple, cheap, abundant, safe and available now. It is possible to have one at the end of your street next month!

This is much more important after storms deny households power for weeks on end.

If, alongside the extra power from domestic producers, there were medium-sized storage batteries the nation would have a massive, robust capability without recourse to the public purse.

In addition, the big power stations would be available to serve cement producers and steelmakers and similar big industries.

The house of the future would have a guaranteed power supply. Of course, this will need an enlightened initiative from Ministries and, heaven forefend, regulators.

Long gone are the days when solar panels had to look like monster dominoes plonked on a roof. Now they can be any colour in lots of textures, weights and finishes and on all quarters of the compass roof and wall alike.

Solar energy sources can be mounted on walls (and they are particularly effective in winter). They can be both solar panels and water heating panels (even located on walls as well) cutting out demand for water heating infrastructure. Solar panels can be very slim and light. But many household services such as lighting can be independent of the roof or grid. There are already solar ovens and solar heat pumps. Solar house warming is already in use even in cold northern climates.

In a few years, the idea that all electric devices need cables to power them will be quaint, even for charging a car.

Having solved the need for externally provided energy, all other devices and desires are now possible.

To get into a home of the future may need digital, retina or face recognition to unlock the door (and a child will not be able to use a cooker because it is controlled by palm prints).

Biometrics or body scanning is already taking off. With Apple and Google Pay, you can now buy your groceries at the touch of a finger. The mobile phone is already a virtual bank when it is scanned to pay a bill (currently up to £100).

Mobile phones are already unlocked by recognising faces and so it's reasonable to imagine biometrics replacing traditional documents, like licences, passports and tickets as our form of ID. Could it be that some 'rooms' in a home will be virtual, private and only accessed using retinal locks (every teen's heaven)?

As an aside, wireless or solar mobile phone charging is practical in preparation for eventual off-grid Climate Change events.

Technology will bridge the gap between the physical and digital worlds. "3D technology and facial recognition tools will allow us to 'download' and apply makeup "fashionable looks" in current demand (in fact a 3D makeup printer already exists which enables users to print out any image they want into wearable makeup), while AI-powered mirrors will scan and analyse our skin and suggest products or ingredients based on results," says Clare Varga, Head of Beauty at forecasting organisation WGSN. Indeed such scanning will also predict the onset of cancer and other ailments.

Houses will need to be able to securely accept self-piloted drones that deliver packages to shoppers' dwellings. IBM patented a coffee delivery drone in 2020 that would not only deliver coffee but would use AI to identify the "cognitive state" of office workers to determine when they need coffee. A young generation will not know where electricity comes from. Induction charging for devices will save having a cat's cradle of wires behind the laptop and printer and power points and plugs will seem antiquated.

Single-use plastics will soon vanish and there could/should be re-cycling technologies in the next generation kitchen.

We learned from the first months of Covid19 that constant digital connectivity (where physical interactions are replaced with digital updates), can increase feelings of social isolation and depression, creating a demand for products and services that help consumers learn to reconnect with themselves and with each other. Enter the Virtual Reality home/office. In China, consumers can already hire a virtual "boyfriend" to go shopping with.

Whole wall screens will be common allowing users to 'sit' in a tropical sea-side chalet with a wall-sized 3D fourth-generation Virtual Reality view of the ocean with a sea breeze and scent of the ocean thrown in. A decade on from the 2020s will be much more exciting than Sony's 2022 VR2 offering. Meta-reality will make such an experience mind-bendingly real.

Perhaps the same wall will extend to a metaverse view to offer a virtual dinner party with lots of guests. Perhaps it will be possible to remotely cook and serve a meal at remote homes? Will that be how you can entertain and feed your elderly relatives on the other side of the country?

Here's a scary idea. What about nearly all the electronic gadgetry in your home able to hold conversations with the occupants and each other. Enter Generative Pre-trained Transformer (GPT-3). It not only already exists, it is already writing press stories and much more. It is often thought that automation will destroy a lot of manual jobs but less is said about white-collar job threats. Computers don't dig holes, they now write like journalists without the hand of man!

There are already organisations seeking to use AI and data to help consumers build smarter wardrobes. Home-based virtual clothes shops, makeup parlours and more will be common and in the home.

Self-guided floor cleaners are already a success. So too is the self-guided mower. There is more by way of automation in the home. We can control cookers, washing machines, tumble dryers, dishwashers and even toasters and kettles from across the world using mobile phone apps. But what if the same Internet of Things (IoT) concept cleaned and dusted valuable heirlooms, made beds, ironed shirts and even emptied the dishwasher?

When self-employment growth started in the UK after the 80's global crisis, there was a sense that people were choosing self-employment because there were no jobs available. It was involuntary. But actually, as the economy has changed, overall self-employment has not fallen. It is continuing to rise.

Oddly, we are told, that many over 50s are falling out of the workforce. Labour market statistics have shown that there are now 180,000 fewer over 50s in work than before the pandemic. 362,000 were unemployed in September 2021, and 3.5 million people aged 50-64 were economically inactive.

The labour shortages created by both Covid-19 and Brexit could be risky for the economy and create skills gaps if older workers do not stay in the workplace.

There are many benefits for employers in retaining and engaging an older workforce, including the skills, experience and organisational knowledge and memory they may have, older workers have highly developed communication skills, they can be adept at problem-solving, and have unique insights and judgements as a result of their experience, and can work well in teams. We are seeing more people working post-retirement age, and wanting to work in a way that they can control.

Is what we see here a long-term trend and if so how does the house of the future cope with middle-aged unemployed and elderly employed people?

Add to that and we find that with the Covid19 lock-down, people discovered a new way of work - working from home. It is a powerful trend. There is a case for re-thinking the nature of work, homes and offices. If more people work from home, do we need offices? Will the trend be growth in re-purposing office blocks into flats and a review of the nature of how offices are converted into dwellings?

Independent workers in the gig economy actually do it because they prefer it.

Perhaps the car-sharing concept for cars will be extended into other areas such as home/office share to provide a social environment.

We could see a dramatic rise of home-based work mutuals and cooperatives and new business models based on the fact that you don't need a headquarters and all the bureaucracy that goes with it. You can just have a 'home located' place and the software to make it all work. And you can start to enjoy the economies of scale that come with that. But we need to do this in a way that is fair to those workers, fair to the market as a whole, and also sustainable in that governments need taxes.

To what extent work and leisure will be mixed is the subject of many studies. But there is no doubt that there are some trends that are obvious.

We tend to think of working from home as an office-based substitution. With the evolution of faster wifi which is moving from 4G to 5G and thence to much faster and higher capacity, the capability and range of activities are going to change what we can do. A combination of high capacity internet, advanced automation and the Internet of Things means that in the next 30 years almost everything that now requires human intervention can be performed remotely.

Everyone can go wherever they want, as long as they get stuff done. The office is a combination of Lifesize, Hangouts, and Virtual Reality depending on whose meeting it is. These technologies also mean that globalisation of work is inevitable. In the future, semi-automated gardening can be controlled by a gardener 3000 miles away on a sun-drenched beach in the Caribbean.

As long as the work gets done and people can be relied on, everybody can manage their time independently and flexibly. What happiness is there in joining work colleagues on a sandy beach virtually, compared to a Metaverse office?

Businesses are hiring more freelancers and contracted organisations a concept that can scale quickly and offers fresh perspectives to established companies. Examples such as building contractors and farming equipment already exist.

Will such automation threaten jobs? Yes!

It seems that skilled jobs are more secure than unskilled ones, but there may be more to the story. Economist, Lucas Puente, believes that less routine jobs are the way to go. In other words, while a radiologist's job is cognitively demanding, it might not be nearly as secure as an electrician's job because the electrician's work is less routine (and therefore less easily replaced by an algorithm).

The skilled craftsmen who is able to repurpose a 19th-century tenement into the 'Passive Housing +' standard will have a more important career than the 'work from home' gig worker.

According to the consulting firm Deloitte, soft skill-intensive occupations will grow 2.5 times faster than the jobs in other felds and account for two-thirds of all jobs by 2030.

The stats on soft skills can be fascinating because they are traditionally seen as inferior to hard skills. This is possible because hard skills in comparison to soft skills have always been easier to evaluate and measure. Even while pursuing higher education, hard skills such as literacy and numeracy are routinely assessed. But what of teamwork, collaboration, and resilience? Not so much!

The nature of work will change and so too must the environment where it is conducted. Is this a room in a house a 'man cave' or a lady studio?

What is more, this will not be a fixed situation. One day it might be at home and later it could be on-site. Team sizes will also change.

Aircraft will use 'green' fuels and will include small 'commuter' 'planes, while electric-powered shopping trolleys will follow us around and perform a range of services and, in some instances, will act as an agent to householders. They will need to be accommodated in the new home.

Self-driving lorries will need managers to handle road trains using a virtual reality console that looks rather like a nuclear submarine control system in a shed at the end of the garden.

Monitoring the human body for ill health at home will be pretty common and will require scans that are not intrusive (there will be no more needles for endless blood tests). What about a brain implant to improve memory or mental capacity? What we can be sure about is that in the clean air of a home, people will be living much longer and so our homes will need to cater for older and more frail people (that does not mean 'less able' - quite the contrary).

Now that an ECG can be done by a mobile phone not to mention pulse, blood pressure, and skin cancer recognition. Automated health care is only a matter of political and medical will.

Ubiquitous wearable or implanted computing devices will continue to be developed and tattoos, nose piercing and clever watches will be soooo yesterday and superseded by embedded technologies. Householders will almost 'feel' their homes from anywhere.

How will these devices be manufactured? In factories. Will 3D printing be good enough to go to the raw materials needed and cut out the middleman? Perhaps we will have 3D printed replacement organs on every high street.

The wider effect is predicted by Mckinsey as follows:

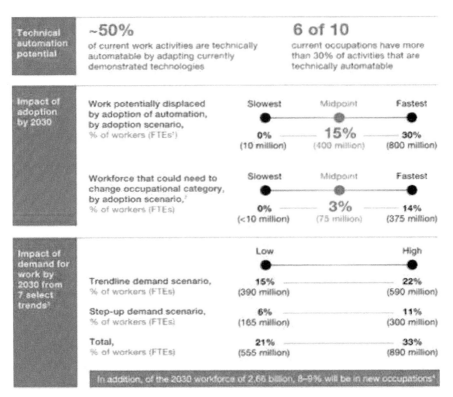

Automation will have a far-reaching impact on the global workforce.

Technical automation potential	~50% of current work activities are technically automatable by adapting currently demonstrated technologies	6 of 10 current occupations have more than 30% of activities that are technically automatable		
Impact of adoption by 2030	Work potentially displaced by adoption of automation, by adoption scenario, % of workers (FTEs¹)	Slowest 0% (10 million)	Midpoint 15% (400 million)	Fastest 30% (800 million)
	Workforce that could need to change occupational category, by adoption scenario,² % of workers (FTEs)	Slowest 0% (<10 million)	Midpoint 3% (75 million)	Fastest 14% (375 million)
Impact of demand for work by 2030 from 7 select trends³		Low		High
	Trendline demand scenario, % of workers (FTEs)	15% (390 million)		22% (590 million)
	Step-up demand scenario, % of workers (FTEs)	6% (165 million)		11% (300 million)
	Total, % of workers (FTEs)	21% (555 million)		33% (890 million)

In addition, of the 2030 workforce of 2.66 billion, 8–9% will be in new occupations⁴

¹ Full-time equivalents
² In trendline labor-demand scenario.
³ Raising incomes; healthcare from aging; investment in technology, infrastructure, and buildings; energy transitions and marketization of unpaid work. Not exhaustive.
⁴ See Jeffrey Lin, "Technological adaptation, cities, and new work," Review of Economics and Statistics, Volume 93, Number 2, May 2011.

McKinsey&Company | Source: McKinsey Global Institute analysis

Workplaces will undoubtedly be different.

At least, all this does not mean the end of the local pub.

Sources and Reference Works Cited

Passivhaus Institut, https://passivehouse.com/. Accessed 30 March 2022.

Passivhaus Institut, https://passivehouse.com/. Accessed 30 March 2022.

"About empty homes." Bradford Council, https://www.bradford.gov.uk/housing/empty-homes/about-empty-homes/. Accessed 30 March 2022.

"Average weekly earnings in Great Britain: November 2021." Average weekly earnings in Great Britain - Office for National Statistics, 16 November 2021, https://www.ons.gov.uk/employmentandlabourmarket/peopleinwork/employmentandemployeetypes/bulletins/averageweeklyearningsi ngreatbritain/november2021. Accessed 30 March 2022.

Brahambhatt, Rupendra, et al. "Welcome to the Age of Wireless Electricity." Interesting Engineering, 1 September 2021, https://interestingengineering.com/welcome-to-the-age-of-wireless-electricity. Accessed 30 March 2022.

"BRE report finds poor housing is costing NHS £1.4bn a year." BRE Group, 9 November 2021, https://www.bregroup.com/press-releases/bre-report-finds-poor-ho using-is-costing-nhs-1-4bn-a-year/?cn-reloaded=1. Accessed 30 March 2022.

Crane, Helen. "Are we heading for a buy-to-let exodus?" This is Money, 29 June 2021, https://www.thisismoney.co.uk/money/buytolet/article-9725329/Ar e-heading-buy-let-exodus.html. Accessed 30 March 2022.

"Dwelling Stock Estimates: 31 March 2019, England." GOV.UK, 31 March 2019, https://assets.publishing.service.gov.uk/government/upload s/system/uploads/attachment_data/file/886251/Dwelling_St ock_Estimate s_31_March_2019_England.pdf. Accessed 30 March 2022.

"Empty housing (England) - House of Commons Library." The House of Commons Library, 21 October 2020, https://commonslibrary.parliament.uk/research-briefings/sn03012/. Accessed 30 March 2022.

"English Housing Survey: headline report." GOV.UK, https://assets.publishing.service.gov.uk/government/upload s/syste m/uploads/attachment_data/file/945013/2019-20_EHS_Headline_ Report.pdf. Accessed 30 March 2022.

"Families and households statistics explained." Office for National Statistics, 15 November 2019, https://www.ons.gov.uk/peoplepopulationandcommunity/bi rthsdeat hsandmarriages/families/articl es/familiesandhouseholdsstatisticsexplained/2019-08-07. Accessed 30 March 2022.

Gibson, Scott. "Balanced Whole-House Ventilation - GreenBuildingAdvisor." Green Building Advisor, 8 October 2021,

https://www.greenbuildingadvisor.com/article/balanced-whole-hou se-ventilation. Accessed 30 March 2022.

Grabham, Dan, and Max Langridge. "Wireless charging explained: Power your iPhone or Android phone wire-free." Pocket-lint, 15 July 2021,

https://www.pocket-lint.com/phones/news/140239-wireless-chargi ng-explained. Accessed 30 March 2022.

Hackl, Cathy. "5G won't be enough: How are telecom companies building the metaverse with Big Tech?" Euronews, 3 March 2022,

https://www.euronews.com/next/2022/03/03/5g-won-t-be-enough- how-are-telecom-companies-building-the-metaverse-with-big-tech. Accessed 30 March 2022.

Hassan, Jennifer. "Greta Thunberg says blah blah blah during climate speech at Italy's Youth4Change." The Washington Post, 29 September2021,

https://www.washingtonpost.com/climate-environment/2021/09/29

/great-thunberg-leaders-blah-blah-blah/. Accessed 30 March 2022.

Higgins, Nick. "This Room Could Wirelessly Charge All Your Devices." Scientific American, 2 September 2021, https://www.scientificamerican.com/article/this-room-could-wirele ssly-charge-all-your-devices/. Accessed 30 March 2022.

"History of house prices in Britain." SunLife, 30 June 2021, https://www.sunlife.co.uk/articles-guides/your-money/the-price-of- a-home-in-britain-then-and-no w/. Accessed 30 March 2022.

"Home - Dr Madeleine Morris." Imperial College London, https://www.imperial.ac.uk/people/m.morris13. Accessed 30 March 2022.

"House of Lords - Building more homes - Select Committee on Economic Affairs." Parliament (publications), https://publications.parliament.uk/pa/ld201617/ldselect/ldec onaf/2 0/2012.htm. Accessed 30 March 2022.

"House prices rise at fastest pace in 17 years." BBC, 29 June 2021, https://www.bbc.co.uk/news/business-57648935. Accessed 29 March 2022.

"How your house may actually earn more money than you." Yorkshire Post, 24 March 2017, https://www.yorkshirepost.co.uk/business/how-your-house-may-ac tually-earn-more-money-you-1781256. Accessed 30 March 2022.

"Jobs lost, jobs gained: What the future of work will mean for jobs, skills, and wages." McKinsey, 28 November 2017, https://www.mckinsey.com/featured-insights/future-of-work/jobs-l ost-jobs-gained-what-the-future-of-work-will-mean-for-jobs-skills- and-wages. Accessed 30 March 2022.

"Legal & General Research Reveals Deepening Housing Crisis." Property Notify, 21 October 2021, https://www.propertynotify.co.uk/news/legal-general-research-reve als-deepening-housing-crisis/. Accessed 30 March 2022.

Linge, Nigel. "5G: what will it offer and why does it matter?" The Conversation, 24 January 2019, https://theconversation.com/5g-what-will-it-offer-and-why-does-it- matter-109010. Accessed 30 March 2022.

Marr, Bernard, and Amy Danise. "The Important Difference Between Web3 And The Metaverse." Forbes, 22 February 2022, https://www.forbes.com/sites/bernardmarr/2022/02/22/the-importa nt-difference-between-web3-and-the-metaverse/. Accessed   30 March 2022.

Mehta, Amar. "UK weather: New Year's Eve could be mildest on record as temperatures expected to reach 15C, the Met Office says." Sky News, 28 December 2021, https://news.sky.com/story/uk-weather-new-years-eve-could-be-mi ldest-on-record-as-temperatu res-expected-to-reach-15c-the-met-office-says-12504593. Accessed 30 March 2022.

Nin, Catherine Sbeglia, and Dean Richmond. "Wi-Fi 7: What is it and when should you expect it?" RCR Wireless News, 27 January 2021, https://www.rcrwireless.com/20210127/network-infrastructure/wi-f i-7-what-is-it-and-when-should-you-expect-it. Accessed 30 March 2022.

"Number of dwellings in England 2001-2020." Statista, 24 June 2021, https://www.statista.com/statistics/232302/number-of-dwellings-in -england/. Accessed 29 March 2022.

O'Hare, Ryan. "Air pollution in England could cost as much as £5.3 billion by 2035 | Imperial News." Imperial College London, 22 May 2018, https://www.imperial.ac.uk/news/186406/air-pollution-england-cou ld-cost-much/. Accessed 30 March 2022.

"Own Your Home | Help to Buy: Equity Loan 2021-2023 - Own Your Home." Help to Buy scheme, https://www.ownyourhome.gov.uk/scheme/help-to-buy-2021-2023 /. Accessed 30 March 2022.

Parker, Fiona. "Meet the homeowners who are the victims of sky-high service charges." This is Money, 3 August 2021, https://www.thisismoney.co.uk/money/markets/article-9858043/M eet-growing-numbers-home-owners-victims-sky-high-service-char ges.html. Accessed 29 March 2022.

"Recent progress of efficient flexible solar cells based on nanostructures." Journal of Semiconductors, http://www.jos.ac.cn/article/id/3ed0e42d-0632-4830-8b47-4f09f1a 2780a?viewType=HTML. Accessed 30 March 2022.

Ryan, Josh. "Is the UK housing bubble about to burst? These are the best and worst scenarios Josh Ryan-Collins." The Guardian, 2 July 2021, https://www.theguardian.com/commentisfree/2021/jul/02/h ousing- bubble-birst-uk-gdp-house-prices-interest-rates-economy. Accessed 29 March 2022.

Schomberg, William, and Michael Holden. "Bank of England's Haldane says UK housing market is on fire." Reuters, 8 June 2021, https://www.reuters.com/world/uk/bank-englands-haldane-says-uk- housing-market-is-fire-2021-06-08/. Accessed 30 March 2022.

Sharman, Laura. "uk - Your authority on UK local government - Charity blasts cost of 'shoddy and expensive' temporary accommodation." LocalGov, 23 October 2020, https://www.localgov.co.uk/Charity-blasts-cost-of-shoddy-

and-exp ensive-temporary-accommoda tion/51292.
Accessed 30 March 2022.

"Specification by Period." Specification by Period,
https://fet.uwe.ac.uk/conweb/house_ages/period/print.htm.
Accessed 30 March 2022.

Spyro, Steph. "Public concern on green issues at highest
level, poll finds." Daily Express, 10 November 2021,
https://www.express.co.uk/news/nature/1519431/cop26-
green-issu es-public-concern-highest-level-poll. Accessed
30 March 2022.

Stevens, John. "Rishi Sunak is to announce cash for new
houses on brownfield land." Daily Mail, 24 October 2021,
https://www.dailymail.co.uk/news/article-10126429/Rishi-
Sunak-a nnounce-cash-injection-tens-thousands-new-
houses-brownfield-lan d.html. Accessed 30 March 2022.

"Tackling the under-supply of housing in England - House
of Commons Library." The House of Commons Library, 4
February 2022,
https://commonslibrary.parliament.uk/research-
briefings/cbp-7671/. Accessed 30 March 2022.

"2019 UK Greenhouse Gas Emissions, Final Figures."
GOV.UK, 2 February 2021,

https://assets.publishing.service.gov.uk/government/upload s/syste m/uploads/attachment_data/fil e/957887/2019_Final_greenhouse_gas_emissions_statistica l_releas e.pdf. Accessed 30 March 2022.

"UK housing: Fit for the future?" Climate Change Committee, https://www.theccc.org.uk/wp-content/uploads/2019/02/UK-housin g-Fit-for-the-future-CCC-2019. pdf. Accessed 30 March 2022.

"Why empty homes matter." Action on Empty Homes, 1 December 2021, https://www.actiononemptyhomes.org/why-empty-homes-matter. Accessed 30 March 2022.

Chapter 5: Planning

Perhaps it's now time to examine the institutions involved in developing our homes. These are not 'homes of the future'. They are homes now for the future.

There is a lot of confusion around. It is important to examine the initiatives of the most influential organisations.

Key among the Chartered institutions affecting housing and Climate Change is the Royal Town Planning Institute (RTPI). The work of its members is heavily criticised as its members produce a conveyor belt of inappropriate planning decisions. Planning outcomes are reputation-crushing. The carbuncle housing estates attached to practically all villages are a classic case in point.

They are cast in a mould of £350,000 new houses supported by an infrastructure that sheds estate-wide rainwater into concrete culverts rushing towards the next flood pinch-point.

The RTPI website says "Planners can embed climate action in local decision making, faster net zero transport, improve urban greening, create affordable housing, smart cities and protect infrastructure from flooding." The word 'can' is a real giveaway. As France, Spain and the UK enjoy weather over 40C it would seem the threat of such temperatures is not a big issue for planners. There is a greater urgency needed.

Victoria Hills, Chief Executive of the RTPI, said: "Planners are a driving force in addressing the climate crisis…." Good. We look forward to it.

The Royal Institute of British Architects (RIBA) is another example. It has set itself a professional challenge.

The '2030 Climate Challenge' is a voluntary initiative for RIBA Chartered Practitioners join to demonstrate their commitment to attempting to meet key sustainability targets on the buildings they design. It includes targets for annual energy use, embodied carbon over the building's lifecycle and annual water use. It provides a stepped approach towards reaching net zero. They are not quite sure if this means net-zero emissions to ameliorate global warming or do these ambitions also reflect the dangers of Climate Change?

The challenge is not mandatory, it is a commitment to show leadership among members' projects and attempt to meet the targets.

The first reaction to such an ambition is to identify that it focuses on mitigating global warming rather than Climate Change alleviation. It is probably unfair to single out RIBA as an exemplar and there are many other similar organisations in the same sort of fix but RIBA is a relevant example.

The RICS - the Royal Institute of Chartered Surveyors - claims: "As a trusted professional body enforcing standards across the built and natural environment, we have an important role to play in shaping a more sustainable world." This is straightforward obfuscation.

One immediately notices that members of this professional body only have to implement its policies on a voluntary basis. The users of the buildings and land they survey can't opt out of Climate Change and need competent advice from advisors who are committed to Climate Change amelioration.

Of course, these institutions aim to influence sustainability by which they mean to design in such a way that future developments will not further aid man's attempts to poison the planet, mainly by reducing the outflow of CO_2 from buildings.

The problem we have is that mitigating global warming is one issue but Climate Change is another but relevant and separate issue and for the most part much closer to home. For dwellings and homes, these twin monsters have to be considered.

The Royal Institution of British Architects (RIBA) has decidedly savvy people among its membership and they must be quite frustrated at the snail's pace of the Institution in demanding higher standards of practice. In its strategy document, it says: "Government must not delay in making strategic Climate Change policy decisions relating to the UK's existing housing stock. It must commit to sustained funding and a package of financial incentive mechanisms for retrofitting, drive standards and regulation, and must support industry in delivering the robust pipeline of skills required to undertake this challenge."

One might ask why wait for the Government to act or, indeed to pay?

In addition to new estates and new buildings, there is much work to be done on retrofitting and renewing old properties to meet future needs (and which is covered elsewhere in this book and is closely argued in the vodcast 'Just Have a Think' - https://www.youtube.com/c/JustHaveaThink).

There is, of course, a difference between mitigating the effects of Climate Change and global warming.

Reducing emissions such as CO_2 to meet the Paris Accord and the 2022 'Conference of the Parties' (COP 26) ambition is essential to reduce the prospect of global warming beyond 1.5 degrees (or more).

So far so good. However, the real problem for users of the RIBA members' design of buildings is in their design for purpose and in the future. Climate Change is a bigger, more urgent and longer term problem for architects. Heat waves, high winds, storms record beating floods (even on high ground and in low rainfall areas) and the threat of township-erasing fires are but a few of the known dangers of Climate Change now and into the future. The need to optimise energy production and develop designs that turn a home into a source of cost saving and revenue is also of concern. Housing needs to change from the old model to a new one that isn't solely a shelter against the cold and woolly mammoths.

Keeping Global Warming to less than 2% is critically important and warming can be mitigated by, among other things, Virtual and Meta Realities in the home but it's long-term. Sweeping flood water out of my inundated brand new house next year is a totally different matter.

So far the RIBA can be applauded for taking an initiative and its associated research. But it does somewhat miss the point. This is very serious if we are going to be able to live with Climate Change and include pollution control in the mitigation of global warming as well as Climate Change. There is more to discuss later.

Royal Charters, granted by the sovereign on the advice of the Privy Council, have a history dating back to the 13th century. They work in the public interest (such as professional institutions and charities) and can demonstrate pre-eminence, stability and permanence in their particular field.

It follows that a member of a Chartered Institution such as the RIBA, RICS and the RTPI has been involved in professional education and the need to meet standards set down by the Institution.

Thus, for example, members are educated and mandated to be good at what they do. It follows that institutions like local authorities should only employ people who are qualified by, and members of, a chartered institution.

In addition, these chartered institutions have a role to play in monitoring best practice and failed performance of members.

This then is a means by which good practice can be applied and monitored without adding costs to local and national government. Perhaps even shifting the current cost of inspectors from government institutions to professional institutions.

Professional institutions have to come up to the mark as well. They have to educate practitioners and provide continuous professional development. Failure of members to come up to the standard is more than a black mark, it should mean loss of membership.

There are some serious standards that can be applied. Poor performance of members should entail the removal of membership from the Chartered Institute and where Institutes are poor at monitoring and enforcing best practices (e.g. removal of ten or more practitioners from their institute for unprofessional activities) they should lose Charter status and after six months of remedial activity can apply to recover Charter status by the Privy Council.

Of course, there is the simple Bill to be passed by government that prohibits public funding to be used (directly or indirectly) where it may be used to reward a practitioner, such as an architect, who does not belong to a chartered institution.

The removal of Charter status from an institution will mean that all members, with few exceptions, would not be allowed to practice where their activities include public funding at any point. This will incentivise members to keep the Chartered institutions up to the mark.

Such policing would save public authorities a lot of money and place good practice in the hands of professionals.

It is easy to be carried away with images of the changes that could be wrought by technologies and Climate Change. It won't be like that. It will take time. The impetus is not yet there even though there are some involved in the construction sector who are well ahead of the curve.

As disaster after disaster echoes across cityscapes at home and abroad, the sluggish acceptance of dramatic change for government and bureaucracy is also going to be a threat. It will take governments several years to get the many involved departments to work together. The civil service empires are devilishly strong and surrounded by walls of regulation that make Dover Castle look like origami.

There will need to be a significant mountain of legislation requiring Parliamentary time going into the next decade. Meantime, there are scientists screaming about the impending crisis on a platform at COP26.

The prospect is a nightmare! There is already a mismatch between government policy and action by the civil service. From Ukraine refugees, to the issue of passports and driving licences performance is dreadful.

Of course, there are some drivers that will put a firework under the mahogany panelled walls of Westminster and Whitehall.

Continuous frightening news at home and abroad will create awareness and some disasters will touch the lives of citizens. The population will sympathise with the plight of those affected and as calamity after calamity drives children, pets and the aged into rescue centres. Mobile phones will continue to record the extent of disasters and fill pages on the internet.

Planning for social disruption both at home and abroad is now essential. Temperatures over 40 C are beginning to have effects in Europe and above 50 C in North Africa is creating population movement. The United Nations High Commissioner for Refugees (UNHCR) reports that an average of 21.5 million people were forcibly displaced each year by sudden onset weather-related hazards between 2008 and 2016, and thousands more from slow-onset hazards linked to Climate Change impacts. In the next few decades, it predicts this will grow seven times.

When planning any new estate or considering renovation and renewal, professionals will have to take into account the prospect of drought lasting many months and storms after weeks or months of rain causing flooding. They need to be catered for.

Senior civil servants will have to prepare the scapegoats and will whisper in the ears of journalists "We have it under control."

The Ministry of Housing, Communities & Local Government, now called "Department for Levelling Up Housing and Communities" will become the dartboard for grassroots activists.

Meantime, over half of the UK population says the government is not doing or spending enough to reduce carbon emissions. As described later in this book, new tools can be used to break down the political red, blue and yellow walls of political elites. Planners giving away planning permissions like sweeties to building speculators will be called to account by hundreds of parish councils and the like across the land.

There is an undertow of public awareness that is already evident in actions and opinion polls. Politicians will have to begin to look at the demands of their constituents. This demand for better planning can continue in a piecemeal way that looks good as did the 2022 Queen's Speech but it will be an opportunity missed and will become issues for future resolution.

The massive financial institutions now with deep property foundations will begin to see they rest on shifting sands.

Economic pressures will also have their place. Planning to invest in the opportunities of debt payment at high interest rates and asset inflation which is the nature of housing today is beginning to look shaky. The big financial institutions are faced with high inflation, and a slowing market. Economic change is not easy to predict but it does look as though there is a need to take it into consideration.

Need or greed.

The great failure of modern planning is the outcome manifest in hundreds of similar houses covering what were once productive fields or havens of self-restoring wildflowers and plants.

107

The houses are mostly built speculatively. Build it and they will come is the mantra for these housing speculators and they have done well out of it. It is a carbuncle building practice.

For those granting planning permission, there is a lot that they can do now to develop better policies and outcomes.

There is also a lot that people who protest against carbuncle development on green fields and on the fringes of towns and villages. In this chapter some of the techniques that can be deployed are outlined to protect localities.

For those involved in granting planning permission and monitoring the quality of the finished product, there are new considerations.

A housing estate built to the highest specification outlined here would be a community asset. It would offer high local housing designed to meet the local need and would help stabilise the local housing market.

A local or parish council that did not insist on the requirements here would be remiss but not necessarily nimby. It should be a responsibility to insist that development was as near as possible future proof.

There are some helpful tools published by the National Association of Local Councils and it is possible to insist that some new rules can be added to Neighbourhood Plans.

Neighbourhood Plans (NPs) give local communities the opportunity to develop a shared vision for their area. Each Plan should be 'positively prepared' and 'add real value' at the local level.

Unlike a parish plan or Village Design Statement, a successful Neighbourhood Plan has statutory weight and status. Once adopted ('made'), it becomes part of the development plan for that area and will be used to help decide planning applications (where relevant). It is the first line of defence against carbuncle building.

The section on 'Where Next for Local Planning' (National Association of Local Councils) is also a useful guide.

However, it's time to invest in a more robust attitude to planning for homes, not just houses. The purpose of the National Model Design Code is to provide detailed guidance on the production of design codes, guides and policies to promote successful design.

The Government's proposal says that all new developments must meet local standards of beauty, quality and design under new rules. Local communities will be at the heart of plans to make sure that new developments in their area are beautiful and well designed. It is a brilliant document. Thorough and quite exciting.

Nicholas Boys Smith, Gail Mayhew, Mary Parsons and Adrian Penfold, the authors have done a great job in the tradition of Government Commissions (45 detailed policy propositions). They are, of course, hampered in their recommendations because of the fast changing environments caused by global warming, Climate Change, fast evolving technologies and events like wars, economic crises, pandemics and global (notably mass) migration.

Their policy proposals are outlined here and are not without their own problems but are a good beginner's guide.

1. Planning: create a predictable level playing field

   This theme asks that beautiful placemaking should be enshrined as a fundamental aim of the planning system, along with greater certainty of planning outcomes, and increased diversity of developers. Looking at the carbuncle housing estates, a cynic might ask if this also applies to the builders of all houses completed per year.

2. Communities: bring the democracy forward

   To improve community engagement in the planning process, in particular on local plans, including the use of a co-design approach, assisted by greater use of digital technology Yet it is not uncommon for the Minister to give planning permission and override the objections of local people and their democratically elected local councillors.

3. Stewardship: incentivise responsibility to the future

   To encourage an approach to development that aims for long-term investment rather than quick profit, in which the values that matter to people – beauty, community, history, landscape – are safeguarded. Walking around new estates, there does not seem to be much by ways of housing to serve the needs of local young marrieds, new graduates, and large families on average incomes.

4. Regeneration: end the scandal of left-behind places

   The Government should commit to ending the scandal of 'left-behind' places and ask 'what will help make these good places to live?' There are two issues here: notably to ensure development to be regenerative and not parasitic and assurance that such renovation does not exclude people already in residence.

5. Neighbourhoods: create places not just houses

   To develop more homes within mixed-use real places at 'gentle density, and change the model of development from 'building units' to 'making places'. This is going to be hard. The ministry is not unused to the 'gentle density' of 20 houses per hectare as, for example in Leeds.

6. Nature: re-green our towns and cities

   Green spaces, waterways and wildlife habitats should be seen as integral to the urban fabric. The Government should commit to a radical plan to plant two million street trees within five years and place a greater focus on access to nature and green spaces. It may be rude to add 'and build 20 houses per hectare'. Equally can one ask: 'who pays'.

7. Management: value planning, count happiness, procure properly

To change the corporate performance and procurement targets of public bodies to take an adequate account of quality. The Home Owners Alliance conducts annual surveys of homeowners. In August 2019 the survey recorded concerns about the quality as "the fastest rising issue" with almost two-thirds (63%) citing housing quality as a serious problem.

There are two big flaws.

1 Devolving so much to Parish Councils without helpful guidance as opposed to laws and regulations scattered across a host of government Ministries.

2 Scores of PDF documents hidden in plain sight in the websites of government departments.

There is always a level of dissent and arm wrestling at parish meetings. Some members are well informed, and others will be quicker than their peers at grasping the implications of recommendations and decisions. It is democracy at work 'red in tooth and claw'. Perhaps it is possible to get '12 good folk and true' to agree on what is a well-designed neighbourhood.

Additionally, Government inspectors have a habit of riding roughshod over local planning decisions.

Turning a couple of acres of farmland into a seven million pound housing estate has its temptations.

The Government policy is as follows:

Communities to be at the heart of plans for well-designed neighbourhoods, to help us Build Back Better.

- Every council to create their own local design code so new developments can reflect what local communities truly want.
- New 'Office for Place' to be set up, to help communities turn these designs into a local standard for all new developments.
- More funding to help communities nominate local historic (drafty, cold, damp, decaying?) buildings for listing.
- Proposals mean local communities will have the power to decide what buildings in their areas should look like, to help the country 'Build Back Better'.

And does this also include the temptation to turn a field into a seven-million pound eyesore (aka carbuncle)?

The process of preparing a local design code, that a parish council will need to follow is based on seven steps outlined in a 34-page code (plus addenda) as revised in 2021 four layers deep into the government's website.

All of these proposals and concepts, and there are lots of them, are well hidden behind a wall of PDF's in a huge website and take more than two full days to read. And, among other similarly interesting documents includes the Tree Preservation Appeal form. Imagine the poor voluntary Parish Councillor having to face all this after getting the kids to do their homework!

In an era of Virtual Reality and Zoom, it seems that there has to be a better way of informing people.

There is another big flaw. Are there enough planning professionals in post? They are important because of both the Housing Crisis and Climate Change Crisis. They have an important role in advising politicians on implementing best practice policies.

Where a developer wants to build there can be some specific applications or new rules.

A mindset that focuses on inflation-proofing has to be thought through. At the same time, there is a need to rethink housing as a concept in a changing climate and at the same time help in the provision of social care.

Nothing can be quite as radical as turning a house into a domestic revenue stream without relying on house-price inflation. Housing then becomes a national asset. Why not?

In developing an estate there are questions about the site such as: generally does it mitigate Climate Change effects. Is it, for example, liable to flood and has it got adequate flood runoff as well as the capability to alleviate downstream inundation? Can buildings on the site be defended from violent storms and long droughts? Is the prospect of electricity brown-outs due to low north sea wind speeds and water shortage because of drought an issue?

Has such an estate got good public services such as roads, water and sewage infrastructure? Is there electric power, estate-wide electricity storage and mesh infrastructure with the ability to accept power generated by the estate's assets and households? Is there effective data cabling and (mesh) wifi supporting the estate? Wifi is now as critical as electricity and has to be treated as such. There is much more to this below.

Individual houses, blocks of flats and other buildings can be designed to generate a lot of electricity. They can store power for when the sun does not shine. Housing estates can also generate large ammouts of electricity and can, automatically, trade in power by offering to sell at times of high demand and buy at time of low demand. Equally small vertical windmills can provide a 24 hour trickle charge as well.

A further development described below offers local distributed battery backup for the National Grid.

Now there are some much bigger questions. Developers and Planning Authorities cheat.

Many developers apply for planning permission and seek an appeal against refusal at the same time.

Approval has been known to be of one design and delivery a completely different specification altogether.

The research into this state of affairs was conducted by Matthew Carmona, a professor at University College, London, whose team has surveyed new housing schemes across the country. It is quite damning.

Before planning permission is given there are a number of questions that can be included in the application.

Examples might include:

What is the developer's provision/contribution of the capital needed to provide additions to schools, public buildings, recreational and sporting services, roads etc. to serve the new residents and the local community. Will this also include optimum solar and wind harvesting, insulation, heat pumps, flood defences and low CO_2 emissions where needed? There is lots more that can be added to this list.

It should be a principle that added houses will create demands for more facilities and that the developer should pay for it. Why should the tax/rate payer have to cough up?

Perhaps the developer has to undertake and publish a comprehensive survey and ensure such facilities are available prior to delivery of accommodation. This is not part of a detailed planning approval; this is an important part of outline permission. It is part of developing communities, new and old.

It has to be true that no outline planning permission should be granted without there being an agreed Local Design Code. If there is no local design code, permission should be refused as a principle. Refused must mean refused! Forever.

There are some elements that can be put into a Neighbourhood Plan and thus can have the protection of the law.

Before considering planning approval public authorities need to be assured on a wide range of subjects in the Neighborhood Plan. Here are some (and in no particular order): Accommodation need

o   Has the prospective developer undertaken a survey using reputable research organisations to ascertain the local housing need within a three/10-mile radius of the site?

○ Did the survey identify the need for accommodation for local 16 to 23-year-old singles living with mum & dad? with an ambition to find independent accommodation?

○ Was there evidence of housing need for the homeless and/or living in cramped and overcrowded or multi-occupation dwellings or other forms of inadequate housing?

○ Did the survey identify social needs including accommodation for the elderly and disabled attached to carer/family homes or independent accommodation nearby on the estate?

○ Will the mix of accommodation (determined by the survey or analysis of lifetime requirement) include limited multi-generation occupancy, including 'granny flats', home offices, games/virtual reality rooms, bicycle storage, boot rooms/outdoor child's toy storage, clothes drying/airing space and EV charging points with car space/garages?

Environment

- Has the prospective developer employed a reputable firm to audit wildlife and carbon capture capability on and near the site?
- What proposals are there to enhance local ecosystems?
- Will shrub and tree planting and other actions aid mitigations of CO_2 and/or methane (CH_4).

- Does the application explain how it will meet important site layout, design and wildlife sustenance and restoration criteria?

Site layout

- Will the layout meet the advice provided by the local police force for optimum security layout (Secured by Design - SBD)?
- Will the site boundary be designed for optimum security and access to the neighbourhood?
- Will the development provide estate and a community-wide secure private (mesh) high speed WiFi network linked to competing satellite and traditional services?
- Is access and egress to the site and approach roads adequate for the new and progressive increase in the use of vehicles, bicycles and pedestrians?
- Does the layout maximise opportunities for energy self-sufficiency from solar and wind harvesting by the proposed properties and estate?
- Is there a proposal for mitigation effects of severe storms, and flooding upstream and downstream?
- Is there a provision on the site for solar, wind and other forms of power harvesting (excluding power generated by domestic dwellings) to supply public services at no cost to the tax and ratepayer?

- Has a provision been made for site-wide green energy network storage (substantial estate located batteries also integrated with the grid).

The money

- Will the provision of such wind and solar lighting and power storage also generate income from the sale of electricity to maintain and service public street furniture and public facilities as a result of the development?
- To what extent will estate-wide revenue from renewables and other sources pay for the provision of public services (e.g. street lighting, rubbish collection, road repair and grass cutting etc.)
- Is there robust provision for the upkeep of the estate after the developer has left?
- Will the mix of dwellings be based on research into actual local housing needs with a range of purchase options? What are they and are they already agreed with the finance providers for: direct purchase, mortgages, leasehold, buy-to-rent, rent and social housing on the same estate?

Maintaining standards

- How will the design, production and finish be warranted to be built with high specification, architect-designed factory-built modules?

- Will the standards set by the International Passive House Association (IPHA) or similar/better be adhered to as the basic standard?
- How will the materials used be warranted low carbon in manufacture and construction?

Mitigating Climate Change

- Will harvesting, storing and cleaning water contribute to helping solve local and national water shortage and treatment issues?
- To what extent will the dwellings be carbon neutral and energy independent (from electricity, water, sewage, and mesh wifi)?
- Will houses and dwellings generate green electricity (using modern solar harvesting products), including charging electric cars and using excess power to the grid or a commercial customer (they often pay more) and derive income from service to the grid for the occupiers?
- How will houses be heated/cooled without recourse to public energy supply?
- Will air purification to remove viruses, bacteria, and pollen plus a range of chemicals and pollutants associated with traffic (such as carbon monoxide, nitrogen oxides, sulphur dioxide, microscopic rubber particles from tyres etc.). Additionally to remove mould spores and viruses such as flu, common cold and

Coronavirus (as available now but upgraded as the technology develops during the estate development)?

And Finally

- Is the housing need being filled by other developments?
- How is the developer going to meet the needs identified in the survey?
- Over what timescale is the need to be addressed/superseded.
- Is the proposed development in excess of the need? If so why?
- Is this plan going to change and if so how and when?
- What is the agreed timetable and what are the sanctions against overrun?

Such questions need to be fully answered and published online and in the local press.

Managing this would seem to be an exhausting process but help is at hand.

Already, manufacturers are developing blockchain implementations that have the potential to help them streamline operations, gain greater visibility into supply chains and track assets with unprecedented precision. This can apply to the planning process as well and can identify where hold-ups are and, at the same time to trace the money spent (plus overspending) and by whom at any time. The range and evolution of these activities was published in the trade magazine Designing Building (27th May 2021 edition).

This is an approach to audit and trust a developer and offering properties that meet Neighbourhood Planning requirements.

Success and failure, visible in the automatic blockchain record can be tested in court and the company directors with their necks on the block. It is important that it is the people/directors who accept responsibility and who have to face sanctions. Suing a company is no more than a higher insurance premium.

However, there is a halfway house in which the developer releases a proportion (20%?) of the properties to residents in the survey area and the other half (but with the same mix, and proportion of dwellings) to home seekers at large and only after the properties offered in the original proposal are finished and occupied. This again has to be a legally binding undertaking.

There are some advantages in such a scheme. The price of at least half the estate dwellings would have to be within the financial reach of the locals.

Typically the cost of accommodation (rent, lease, loans and part ownership etc.) has to be no more than 25% of the household's principal wage earner. There is no point in providing homes for people that just pushes them into poverty.

If government want to subsidise the house building sector then here is the opportunity. It can extend the scope of the Social Housing Regulation Bill and the renting White Paper and extend the development of purchase options. But why the government should want to sprinkle money over the housing sector is a complete mystery. It is a big sector and has lots of money of its own.

So, it's fun to think of housing that does not upset the natives. The Neighbourhood Plans, where there is a legal framework to add authority to such activity, will help remove the deep suspicion of speculative property developers across society.

Hey! All you campaigning groups, parish councillors and local MP's, ask the questions outlined above. Make sure the answers are public to inform electors who have a sanction that is democratically powerful.

Perhaps it is time for planning campaign groups to ask, in public, if there is a survey that identifies local actual housing needs. Most councils could not afford to do this every time a planning application is submitted but property developers can and should.

The planning authorities can then specify what will be included in such surveys but not pay for them.

As we go through more of the opportunities now available for the development of estates, there will be even more considerations.

But just meeting local housing needs is a top priority.

With such an array of issues resolved before a planning application is submitted, as a matter of routine, the time it takes to complete the planning approval process can be reduced to weeks instead of months or, more often, years. Driving through the process is governed by the results of the survey and thus a timescale is part of the planning process. No more holding on to land in the hope that land price inflation will save the developer from financing property. Under this approach to development, land stops being a bank and is used to serve the nation's housing needs.

Stuffing dwellings into small plots is a problem.

The need to build houses has led local authorities and developers into a habit of stuffing as many dwellings into a space as possible.

It often leads to not just on-street parking but on-pavement parking as well. There is a need, in such circumstances, to sacrifice a dwelling in order to provide parking (and EV charging points, grocery delivery lockers and other needs) for residents. Such places also can go upwards and provide community services in the storeys above ground level. And it would be fun to have space for delivery drones.

This thinking can also be applied to tower block living (including converted offices and warehouses). Wide corridors to accommodate wheelchairs are a typical need but so too is space for play both for children and grown-ups. Have all flats and houses access and room to (easily) park a bike, pram, wheelchair, shoes, boots, umbrellas and grampy's walking frame plus an outdoor cupboard for skis, paddleboard, wet suit and all those things that need to be stored for occasional use? If not, why not? All homes need such accommodation. There is a need to solve such demands for domestic space.

These are sacrifices of space to make life more bearable and it will reduce housing density but is a proper sacrifice. The difference between houses and homes.

It is time to take a long look at the opportunities available to us to meet them now.

Planning needs to deliver faster, with less bureaucracy to meet needs and create more homes faster. At present planners are failing the population.

Sources and References

RTPI | Home, https://www.rtpi.org.uk/. Accessed 31 March 2022. 2030 Climate Challenge FAQs, https://www.architecture.com/about/policy/climate-action/2030-cli mate-challenge/faqs. Accessed 2 April 2022.

EuroPHit | Retrofitting for the energy revolution, one step at a time, https://europhit.eu/. Accessed 2 April 2022.

Privy Council, https://privycouncil.independent.gov.uk/. Accessed 6 April 2022.

National Association of Local Councils (NALC), https://www.nalc.gov.uk/. Accessed 6 April 2022.

Secured By Design, https://www.securedbydesign.com/. Accessed 6 April 2022.

Secured By Design, https://www.securedbydesign.com/. Accessed 6 April 2022.

Welcome to the Zero Carbon Hub website! | Zero Carbon Hub, https://www.zerocarbonhub.org/. Accessed 6 April 2022.

Fuller, Gary. "For hydrogen power to be a climate solution, leaks must be curbed." The Guardian, 17 June 2022, https://www.theguardian.com/environment/2022/jun/17/pol lutionw atch-hydrogen-power-climate-leaks. Accessed 17 June 2022.

"All new developments must meet local standards of beauty, quality and design under new rules." GOV.UK, 30 January 2021,

https://www.gov.uk/government/news/all-new-developments-must- meet-local-standards-of-beau ty-quality-and-design-under-new-rules. Accessed 6 April 2022.

"Blockchain in manufacturing - IBM Blockchain." IBM,

https://www.ibm.com/blockchain/industries/manufacturing. Accessed 6 April 2022.

"Building a Transparent Supply Chain." Harvard Business Review, https://hbr.org/2020/05/building-a-transparent-supply-chain. Accessed 6 April 2022.

guide, step. "Neighbourhood Planning » Babergh Mid Suffolk." Mid Suffolk DistrictCouncil,

https://www.midsuffolk.gov.uk/planning/neighbourhood-planning. Accessed 6 April 2022.

guide, step. "PUBLICATIONS." National Association of Local Councils,

https://www.nalc.gov.uk/publications#what-next-%E2%80%A6. Accessed 6 April 2022.

"JOE DOUCET x PARTNERS JDXP." JOE DOUCET x PARTNERS JDXP,

https://joedoucet.com/windturbinewall/. Accessed 31 March 2022.

Konstantatos, Gerasimos. "New efficiency record set for ultrathin solar cells." University College London, 15 February 2022, https://www.ucl.ac.uk/news/2022/feb/new-efficiency-record-set-ult rathin-solar-cells. Accessed 1 April 2022.

Limb, Lottie. "Solar panels built from waste crops can make energy without direct light." Euronews, 26 February 2022, https://www.euronews.com/green/2022/02/19/solar-panels-built-fr om-waste-crops-can-make-energy-without-direct-light. Accessed 1 April 2022.

"List of organisations in the United Kingdom with a royal charter." Wikipedia, https://en.wikipedia.org/wiki/List_of_organisations_in_the_United _Kingdom_with_a_royal_chart er. Accessed 2 April 2022.

"National Model Design Code." GOV.UK, 20 July 2021, https://www.gov.uk/government/publications/national-model-desig n-code. Accessed 6 April 2022.

Beecham, Richard. "Massive 785-home Wetherby plans reviewed." Harrogate Advertiser, 14 March 2022, https://www.harrogateadvertiser.co.uk/news/people/massiv e-785-h ome-wetherby-plans-reviewed-3609665. Accessed 17 June 2022.

"Neighbourhood planning." GOV.UK, https://www.gov.uk/guidance/neighbourhood-planning--2. Accessed 6 April 2022.

"Neighbourhood planning." GOV.UK, https://www.gov.uk/guidance/neighbourhood-planning--2. Accessed 6 April 2022.

"Officers / Members of the British Polling Organisation." British Polling Council, https://www.britishpollingcouncil.org/officers-members/. Accessed 6 April 2022.

"Royal Charters." Privy Council, https://privycouncil.independent.gov.uk/royal-charters/. Accessed 2 April 2022.

"Solar Tiles Now a Reality in Kenya." Construction Review Online, 5 May 2020, https://constructionreviewonline.com/company-reviews/solar-tiles- now-a-reality-in-kenya/. Accessed 1 April 2022.

Wilson, Wendy. "New-build housing: construction defects - issues and solutions (England) - House of Commons Library." The House of Commons Library, 17 January 2022, https://commonslibrary.parliament.uk/research-briefings/cbp-7665/

. Accessed 17 June 2022.

Tate, Lesley. "National shortage of planning officers holding up improvements to Craven's development services." The Craven Herald, 3 February 2022,

https://www.cravenherald.co.uk/news/19897877.national-shortage- planning-officers-holding-imp

rovements-cravens-development-services/. Accessed 6 April 2022.

"Technology." Ambri, https://ambri.com/technology/. Accessed 6 April 2022. "Time For Trust: How blockchain will transform business and the economy." PwC,

https://www.pwc.com/gx/en/industries/technology/publicati ons/blo ckchain-report-transform-busin ess-economy.html. Accessed 6 April 2022.

"Untitled." Rainwater Harvesting, https://www.rainwaterharvesting.co.uk/wp-content/uploads/2021/1

1/rainwater-harvesting-information.pdf. Accessed 6 April 2022.

Wall, Tom. "Serious design flaws in many housing estates, report claims." The Guardian, 19 January 2020, https://www.theguardian.com/society/2020/jan/19/housing-giants-p ut-profit-before-peoples-needs-report-reveals. Accessed 6 April 2022.

"What is an eco house?" Design for Me, 6 January 2022, https://designfor-me.com/project-types/self-build/what-is-an-eco-h ouse/. Accessed 2 April 2022.

"What Is Blockchain Technology? How Does It Work?" Built In, https://builtin.com/blockchain. Accessed 6 April 2022.

Chapter 6: The Estate

Who then, needs homes?

Some sleep rough with no access to housing. Those in inadequate accommodation often lack basic needs with shared cooking, toilet, and not even space for a bicycle. The next stage up is rented but crowded, often multi-household accommodation that needs attention. Public social housing lists are long and often at the fringes of affordability (typically with rents just over the State Support and pension levels).

Public, commercial and Housing Trust suppliers of rented accommodation typically cost tenants more than they can afford.

Social housing is charged chiefly at more than 30% of standard national retirement pension income. There are several complex routines to get added state support and costly state bureaucracy. Without a nod and a wink, the average 75-year-old would find the process daunting, if not impossible. In addition to such needs, the rented sector and private housing sector are, all too often, at a point where the cost is right at the edge of affordability, leaving tenants homeless, on the edge of starvation and even unable to support young families.

The issues were outlined in the 2017 Government White Paper, and housing statistics don't offer much hope.

The ambition is to:

- Build suitable homes in the right places.
- Build them faster.
- Widen the range of builders and construction methods.
- 'Help people now', including investing in new affordable housing and preventing homelessness.

A typical approach like "Build Homes, Build Jobs, Build Innovation: A Blueprint for a Housing Led Industrial Strategy" (Mike De'Ath and Mark Farmer September 2020) offers some radical ideas too, supported by sound research.

Heriot-Watt University research proposes 145,000 affordable homes should be built annually for the next five years, of which 90,000 a year should be for 'social rent. This is the lowest-cost housing that councils and housing associations provide, with rents tied to local incomes. In recent times fewer than 7,000 new homes a year have been created in this category in England.

Enter 'the estate. We understand the building estate and the council housing estate and estate in the suburbs, But there are other estates. They can be Belgravia or the tenements near the canal. They can be large and small but they are a cohesive group of homes.

For the future, there is a need for a range and mix of dwellings to include multiple occupancies, purpose-built 'granny' annexes, and housing for the homeless, deprived and disabled. Young person accommodation and (differently) 'newly wed' dwellings aimed at keeping communities together. Children who live with their families leave home, on average, at around 23 years old. These people also need to be considered in the development and re-development of housing estates and local communities.

In addition, why should new homes be offered at the cost of more than 25% of the income of the principal wage earner? Furthermore, this rule will need to be reflected in the sales agreement in any future sale.

There still has to be provision for ordinary folk, rich and poor, to buy the kind of house they want to call home.

All such thinking has a beneficial impact on the provision and cost of social services including housing, family-assisted and independent residential care and support for independent living.

There is need for recreation space for children and adults and local facilities such as local shops, meeting halls, places to practice religions, see a medical robot and space for public transport drones. The most famous drone taxi currently is Ehang 184, the world's first drone-taxi.

This kind of policy goes hand in hand with social care in the community and community cohesion.

A home partly used as an office is now common in most cities and rural towns and villages. The City of London has plans to build 1,500 new homes in former office blocks left vacant due to the pandemic but are these monoculture estates? Is there a better, more inclusive, option?

Since 2015, property developers have been allowed to convert offices into apartments without getting full planning permission, under a system called permitted development rights - and that policy now applies to shops and warehouses too. But are these dwellings meeting local needs? Are the poor, elderly, big families, and home hopefuls all being catered for? Are they meeting needs or just a speculative adventure on the part of owners? Many converted dwellings are tiny.

Even smaller than two and a half cars which is the minimum space advised by the government.

Pathetic, dehumanising and a built-in health hazard. Where is the development survey?

In a city like Leeds the university student need is met with localised and tiny flats. They edge out other types of residents who have been cast aside by the planners and university authorities. Perish the thought that a student should live in a community with working-class Tories next door!

What then of Climate Change. Cities are already hotter than the countryside. More people die from heat causes that are exacerbated by small accommodation and it's getting worse: about 4000 per year. Many residents need additional space for home offices. Some have changing circumstances such as a new baby. In a tiny box, life can be really miserable. The need for a higher standard and bigger dwellings is essential. It does mean fewer residents for the owners (and less by way of rent) of repurposed houses, warehouses and reconstituted housing estates. But it is essential or will more people be forced to live in ever-increasing housing poverty.

In the areas that are representative of local communities, the mix of people will be those who have difficulty paying even just 25% of earnings as rent each week. Many do not have domestic budgeting skills.

Where appropriate, provision will have to be available to collect rents/mortgages and rates through sequestration of public financial support such as pensions and social security payments ('social rent') to help such people manage their finances. This provision ensures a steady revenue stream for investors and offers a roof over the head of all sectors in our communities. Such built-in help means that all housing can be financed without recourse to eviction. Under the new provision for tenants to have residential security for four months the ability to recover rents this way is really needed if the rented sector is to survive.

Who owns the street

So many stakeholders suffer heat-related deaths, 2000 homes flooded and sinkholes caused by drought and storm are already happening. Increasingly it is becoming commonplace and is an urban war in the making.

A dwelling is not one household's angst. It belongs to the community. It is a community that has to respond. Such a community has to take on a Climate Change sized range of responsibilities.

There is no doubt that the many stakeholders will have to come together and work positively as a team.

The range of stakeholders is large and diverse. It's not just sorting out which utility can take a turn at digging up the road especially when it has just had new kerbstones, or tamac laid. It is beyond those who replaced the bulb in a street light, painted yellow lines, emptied the bins and places the heavy hand of the law on County Lines crooks. The facilitators that provide services for the underprivileged and social services, education and recreation also have an interest. Social groups also have a say. The religious, sporting and other societies have a keen interest too. Close interest and involvement will also come from the public, private and local moneylenders. All these elements (and there are many more) have a stake in an estate or locality and each dwelling.

Central to this list are, of course, residents and their dependants (old and young). They have the power of being a campaigning resident, a voter, and a supportive and/or angry voice. They can also be wealthy or financially challenged including pensioners (or with other government-funded incomes) and they pay rent/or other finance and, additionally, rates. They may even be dependent on house price inflation just to fund a pension.

Most people would be surprised to find out how many people and organisations have a stake in their homes and location.

The Climate Change Estate

Such groups need to exist and have to be encouraged.

It would seem that a group of Climate Change Citizens should be able to combine under a single organisational umbrella. This might be a quasi-legal entity or a group supported by the local or national government or in a legal framework. This is not a replacement for local democratic institutions like parish councils. A 'Climate Change Estate' could be run as a co-operative or as a private closed estate.

Such a group would need to be able to undertake joint actions affecting them all in an unbreakable relationship. Thus, for example, the water, power, utilities and communication entities could work together as a single entity within an estate.

Such an estate may have to identify who should be stakeholders. Alternatively, this will be an entity with its stakeholders all being shareholders but the underlying principle for all must be the mitigation of Climate Change events and contribution to Global Warming mitigation.

Because the efforts of the Estate have this dual aim (Climate Change, of course, being the most important), it will have to offer a contribution to its stakeholders. At the end of the day property owners will not want to be more beholden to the Climate Change Estate beyond their financial contribution or ambitions.

There is also a need to insure against bad practices. The Place Alliance advocates for place quality. It is focused on the idea that through evidence and collaboration quality of place becomes an everyday national and local priority. Its research shows how ghastly a lot of development has been and is even today. This has to change and it is up to the government to inject teeth into existing legislation and rules.

The government would, of course, like to control Climate Change estates are, after all, politicians. However, they can create an environment for such estates to thrive. The responsibility can be shifted from the government to the, reformed, professions guided by the planning approvals based on the last chapter.

A community will have many roles and not all streets or estates will be the same.

One of the big opportunities is the ability to generate income in its own right. A substantial part of this income may be from rented and leasehold properties but also can come from selling access, services, electricity (grid and commercial customers), and estate management services (such as automated street cleaning etc.) to external bodies.

For example, there may be a pond or pool that can be a leisure installation but also a reservoir that can collect water from the homes and sell it to Water Utilities in times of (more frequent) drought but might also provide water (for a fee) to estate residents for a car cleaning facility and to water plants.

Today a lot of hydrogen is produced using solar power. It is valuable and a source of income for homes and estates. It can be used as a form of energy storage and facilities for generation are readily available.

Street lighting where lamp posts combine horizontal or vertical windmills, solar panels and batteries are a source of income. The cost of street lighting is thereby eliminated and there will be power to spare to store in the large local community battery, a commercial customer or to charge electric vehicles. Such street lights can also include security cameras/monitors (the size of a grain of salt?) and have sensors that act as fire alarms and even sense the presence of drugs on a person walking by.

A local community might also have green areas and play areas that not only include trees to capture carbon but also vertical windmill sculptures to generate a non-stop trickle of more electricity to light up playgrounds and other public facilities.

A layer of piezoelectric crystals under the asphalt have the property to convert mechanical energy into an electric voltage as they're distorted by passing traffic. This is yet another opportunity to generate income. Bricks that are the same colour all the way through are a great way to embed road markings and can be used for a wide range of applications. They never have to be repainted and can be porous to allow rainwater through.

Housing communities can also offer car-sharing services and landing pads for automated cargo drones (shopping delivery drones to most of us). In due course, it may also need to be able to provide facilities for airborne cars.

Many such estates will also provide homes and refuge for the more deprived. These can be managed by such enterprises.

Developing a modern housing estate has several considerations that are not usual today.

The time has come to separate the Housing Estate from the developer and builder.

There is no longer money to spray onto local authorities for services. This means that housing streets and estates will have to be maintained as a single unit providing its own services for its own communities and at a much-reduced cost to the public purse.

The developer will no longer be the housebuilder (the fact is that most developers sub-contract such work anyway). The developer will be responsible for structuring site management and ensuring house sales and revenues are provided as high-quality, modern, affordable and appealing homes. An estate will comprise revenue-generating homes that will help fund the accommodation and maintain affordability at 25% of the principal occupier's income.

The builder is no longer an on-site house builder because future carbon neutral and flexible accommodation is best built in a factory and transported to the site where specialist contractors complete the groundwork. One or two deliveries instead of hundreds of lorries and vans.

All this means is that estates need to be self-funding so that when the developer has left, it will be able to maintain the aesthetic, infrastructure and layout.

Developing this way means that there has to be a range of accommodation. The mix of the community (based on housing need research) will have to be reflected in the nature and design of housing estates of, say, more than half a dozen new dwellings. It follows that the price of housing will have to be a consideration as well.

The historical experience is telling.

The West Northants District Council (WNDC) was initially established in 2004 with a housing delivery focus. Still, it encountered difficulties, and after five years – and in the aftermath of the financial crisis - its focus shifted towards regeneration projects. A review of WNDC by John Moores University noted that: "By common consent it had a very difficult start, as the area simply wasn't prepared for a massive amount of housing development in terms of infrastructure, planning policy and community support."

We have to do away with the idea of 'one size fits all'. Monoculture development is daft and costly.

In Wrexham, a council housing estate was so unpopular that it had to be destroyed.

The next generation housing/local estate seems like a good and inexpensive place to live.

Representative mixed communities, public services self-financed, local harvesting of energy in public spaces (e.g. solar, wind power and green hydrogen etc.) are interesting ideas. Estate-wide revenues to maintain the aesthetic of the housing estate and replace services generally provided by

144

local authorities. Including security 'designed in' using advice from the Association of Chief Police Officers Crime Reduction Initiatives (ACPO CRI) add comfort to many.

Provision for the local community to (automatically) monitor speeding vehicles with beefed-up speeding fines can be sequestered from drivers and paid to the local parish council for road (pothole) maintenance and improvement would serve a number of purposes.

Public transport and connections to essential services are often a responsibility passed on to the local government agencies. Provision for present and future services might even include locally produced green energy, driverless taxis, and shopping delivery robots sound like a good idea too.

The housing community of the future will be different. It will be designed for the locality and local needs. It will generate revenues to maintain a beautiful environment and yet will be a revolution in its ability to help people lead healthier lives in a more spacious environment and will turn an expensive drain on the family purse into an asset that generates income.

Sources and References

Saule Technologies – Inkjet-Printed Perovskite Solar Cells,https://sauletech.com/. Accessed 1 May 2022.

Bespoke, Cost-effective Modular & Portable Buildings from Springfield Modular | Springfield,

https://www.spring-field.co.uk/. Accessed 11 May 2022.

Saule Technologies – Inkjet-Printed Perovskite Solar Cells,https://sauletech.com/. Accessed 11 May 2022.

"About the care system - Become." Become Charity, https://www.becomecharity.org.uk/care-the-facts/about-the-care-sy stem/. Accessed 30 April 2022.

"Best practice review of community action on Climate Change."

Centre for Sustainable Energy,

https://www.cse.org.uk/projects/view/1108. Accessed10 May 2022.

Buck, Rhiannon. "Can traffic generate electricity?" BBC Science Focus Magazine,

https://www.sciencefocus.com/future-technology/can-traffic-gener ate-electricity/. Accessed 30 April 2022.

"Buying homes in Private Estates." Carter Bells, https://www.carterbells.co.uk/notices/buying-homes-private-estates /. Accessed 30 April 2022.

Carrington, Damian. "Converted offices pose 'deadly risk' in heatwaves, experts warn." The Guardian, 1 August 2021,

https://www.theguardian.com/society/2021/aug/01/converte d-offic es-pose-deadly-risk-in-heatwa

ves-experts-warn. Accessed 30 April 2022.

Chai, Wesley. "What is a wireless mesh network? WMNs Explained." TechTarget,

https://www.techtarget.com/searchnetworking/definition/wi reless- mesh-network. Accessed 11 May 2022.

Chattha, Kamran. "Is wind power from a moving car a wasteful method of generating electricity?" Quora,

https://www.quora.com/Is-wind-power-from-a-moving-car-a-waste ful-method-of-generating-electricity. Accessed 30 April 2022.

"Cities and Local Action to Combat Climate Change." UNFCCC, https://unfccc.int/topics/education-youth/youth-engagement/global

-youth-video-competition/glob

al-youth-video-competition-2019/cities-and-local-action-to-combat-climate-change. Accessed 10 May 2022.

"Climate Change risk assessment." Climate Change Committee, https://www.theccc.org.uk/publicationtype/0-report/09-climate-cha nge-risk-assessment/. Accessed 10 May 2022.

"Communities vs Climate Change: the power of local action." New Local, 20 October 2021, https://www.newlocal.org.uk/publications/communities-climate-ch ange/. Accessed 10 May 2022.

De'Ath, Mike. "Build Homes, Build Jobs, Build Innovation." HTA Design,   21   September   2020, https://www.hta.co.uk/news-description/major-report-calls-buildin g-75000-new-modular-homes-y   ear-create-50000-new-jobs. Accessed 30 April 2022.

"Food banks provide more than 2.1 million food parcels to people across the UK in past year, according to new figures released by the Trussell Trust." The Trussell Trust, 27 April 2022, https://www.trusselltrust.org/2022/04/27/food-banks-provide-more -than-2-1-million-food-parcels-to-people-across-the-uk-in-past-yea r-according-to-new-figures-released-by-the-trussell-trust/. Accessed 10 May 2022.

"Generating power every time you hit the road." Rutgers CAIT, 4 March 2019, https://cait.rutgers.edu/generating-power-every-time-you-hit-the-ro ad/. Accessed 1 May 2022.

"Housing supply requirements across Great Britain for low- income households and homeless people." Need to set up Multi-Factor   Authentication?   Visit our MFA guidance,

https://pure.hw.ac.uk/ws/files/24741931/HousingSupplyMa
y2019. pdf. Accessed 10 May 2022.

Hughes, Alex. "Scientists build full-colour camera the "size
of a grain of salt."" BBC Science Focus Magazine, 8
December 2021,
https://www.sciencefocus.com/news/scientists-build-full-
colour-ca mera-the-size-of-a-grain-of-salt/. Accessed 30
April 2022.

"Humanity's Broken Risk Perception Reversing Global
Progress in 'Spiral of Self-destruction.'" UNFCCC, 26 April
2022,
https://unfccc.int/news/humanity-s-broken-risk-perception-
reversin g-global-progress-in-spiral-of-self-destruction.
Accessed 30 April 2022.

"Insights Community action for the environment." The
National Lottery Community Fund,
https://www.tnlcommunityfund.org.uk/insights/community
-action- for-the-environment. Accessed 10 May 2022.

"IP Connect UK - Private IP VPN." BT Business,
https://business.bt.com/products/networking/ip-connect/.
Accessed 11 May 2022.

Kenber, Billy. "Developer's flat is smaller than a taxi |
News." The Times, 12 July 2019,
https://www.thetimes.co.uk/article/developer-s-flat-is-
smaller-than- a-taxi-8xnthx63t. Accessed 10 May 2022.

Laver, Nicola. "Privacy in Your Own House: Who can enter your home? - InBrief.co.uk." In Brief, https://www.inbrief.co.uk/property-law/who-can-enter-your-house/

. Accessed 30 April 2022.

Magnus, Ed. "Are we on the cusp of a rental crisis? Available homes at record lows." This is Money, 31 March 2022, https://www.thisismoney.co.uk/money/buytolet/article-10664537/ Are-cusp-rental-crisis-Available-properties-record-lows.html. Accessed 30 April 2022.

"Major acceleration of homegrown power in Britain's plan for greater energy independence." GOV.UK, 6 April 2022, https://www.gov.uk/government/news/major-acceleration-of-home grown-power-in-britains-plan-for-greater-energy-independence. Accessed 10 May 2022.

""Misguided and out of touch" CSE responds to government's Energy Strategy." Centre for Sustainable Energy, 7 April 2022, https://www.cse.org.uk/news/view/2686. Accessed 10 May 2022.

"New digital service to improve home energy performance." GOV.UK, 30 September 2020, https://www.gov.uk/government/news/new-digital-service-to-impr ove-home-energy-performance. Accessed 30 April 2022.

"Our Impact." ilke Homes, https://ilkehomes.co.uk/our-impact/. Accessed 11 May 2022.

"Place QualityResearch." Place Alliance, https://placealliance.org.uk/research/. Accessed 30 April 2022.

"Place Value Wiki - B1. Street layout and crime." Google Sites, https://sites.google.com/view/place-value-wiki/society/b1-street-la yout-and-crime. Accessed 11 May 2022.

"Planning Out Crime in New Development." Bury Council, https://www.bury.gov.uk/CHttpHandler.ashx?id=2233&p= 0. Accessed 1 May 2022.

Power, Anne. "Hunger pains: The growing need for food banks is just the tip of the iceberg." LSE Blogs, 12 December 2014, https://blogs.lse.ac.uk/politicsandpolicy/hunger-pains-rise-of-the-f ood-bank/. Accessed 30 April 2022.

Quach, Georgina. "Fastest rent rise in five years adds to concerns over UK cost of living crisis." The Guardian, 16 February 2022, https://www.theguardian.com/money/2022/feb/16/fastest-rent-rise- in-five-years-uk-cost-of-living-crisis-house-price. Accessed 30 April 2022.

"Regen and the Electricity Storage Network – Written evidence (BAT0027)." UK Parliament Committees, 29 March 2021, https://committees.parliament.uk/writtenevidence/25310/pdf/. Accessed 30 April 2022.

"Research National Housing Audit."Place Alliance, https://placealliance.org.uk/research/national-housing-audit/. Accessed 10 May 2022.

"The Retrofit Playbook." UK Green Building Council, 1 February 2021, https://www.ukgbc.org/wp-content/uploads/2021/02/Retrofit-Playb ook.pdf. Accessed 30 April 2022.

Smith, Nicholas Boyes. "BUILD HOMES, BUILD JOBS, BUILD INNOVATION: A BLUEPRINT FOR A HOUSING LED INDUSTRIAL STRATEGY." HTA Design, 1 September 2020, https://www.hta.co.uk/storage/app/media/build-homes-build-jobs-b uild-innovation.pdf. Accessed 30 April 2022.

Smith, Nicholas Boyes. "BUILD HOMES, BUILD JOBS, BUILD INNOVATION: A BLUEPRINT FOR A

HOUSING LED INDUSTRIAL STRATEGY." HTA Design, 1 September 2020,
https://www.hta.co.uk/storage/app/media/build-homes-build-jobs-b uild-innovation.pdf. Accessed 10 May 2022.

Taylor, Brogan. "About the size of a London flat | National Statistical." National Statistical, 21 February 2020, https://blog.ons.gov.uk/2020/02/21/about-the-size-of-a-london-flat/
. Accessed 10 May 2022.

"Title: APPG on Sure Start Children's Services." Local Government
Association,
https://www.local.gov.uk/sites/default/files/documents/plan ning-ou t-crime-pdf-3--487.pdf. Accessed 1 May 2022.

"Traces of Illicit Drugs Found in Public Air." WIRED, 16 December
2011,
https://www.wired.com/2011/12/illegal-drugs-air-quality/. Accessed 30 April 2022.

"Urban Green Energy Wind and Solar Powered Street Lamp." Inhabitat, 13 July 2009, https://inhabitat.com/hybrid-wind-solar-street-lamps/streetlamp_ne ighborhood-hawt_1/. Accessed 10 May 2022.

"Water - what is going on?" Dieter Helm, 13 September 2021, http://www.dieterhelm.co.uk/natural-capital/water/floods-water-co mpany-regulation-and-catchme

nts-time-for-a-fundamental-rethink-2/. Accessed 1 May 2022.

Webb, Abby. "Working from home statistics UK [Updated for 2022] — The Home Office Life."

The Home Office Life, 19 February 2022, https://thehomeofficelife.com/blog/work-from-home-statistics.

Accessed 10 May 2022.

"What Are Mesh Networks and Are They a Viable Internet Alternative? - Cordcutting.com." CordCutting.com, 10 December 2021, https://cordcutting.com/isp/mesh-network/. Accessed 30

April 2022.

"What is a housing co-operative?" Community Led Homes, https://www.communityledhomes.org.uk/what-housing-co-operative. Accessed 30 April 2022.

Williams, Francesca. "Storm Arwen: Why power cuts left people unable to phone for help." BBC, 12 December 2021, https://www.bbc.co.uk/news/uk-england-cumbria-59564480. Accessed 30 April 2022.

"Wind And Solar Hybrid Street Light System." Wind turbine_Solar panel_Battery_LED luminaire_Wind and solar hybrid power generation system, https://www.urilic.com/solution-item-169001.html. Accessed 30April 2022.

"Yellow... - Yellow Brick Road Properties- Properties for Sale." Facebook, https://www.facebook.com/YellowBrickRoadProperties/photos/a.1 594202934025837/159420287 0692510/?type=3. Accessed 30 April 2022.

Chapter 7: A Construction

Building houses today (with a few exceptions) just adds to the problem of environmental damage.

We still use bricks as they did in the first city of Çatalhöyük in Anatolia 9000 years ago.

Using brick and cement modern houses are accountable for the largest used share of energy consumption but the essential use of the brick remains. How we make them tells a story of Global Warming.

Concrete, bricks, tiles, roadways and diesel-powered site machinery are planet killers. They produce CO_2 by the tonne. The ground once absorbed rainwater and fixed greenhouse gases but is now covered in impermeable asphalt and concrete. So-called 'energy efficient' new buildings produce 1.45 tonnes of CO_2 per year and use a lot of electricity per annum.

However, the increase in 'energy-efficient buildings is growing. Bricks have a less popular future.

New house energy performance statistics show a 16% improvement in 2021. But, compared with the Passive House Standard which is not without its limitations, the UK building standard has been set at a very low level. Bricks and cement are still seen on almost every building site.

We have to accept that there are major changes taking place such as drought, heat waves, rising sea levels, melting glaciers and warming oceans not to mention fires and intense storms. That means that the normal house built in 2022 is doomed to be blown away sometime soon.

A population leaning towards improved protection and mitigation of Climate Change is now a major political influence and ranks third among the most important issues for the population at large.

As we will see, the evidence around us and regarding the science now available, there is no doubt that architects, builders and renovators have to make big strides to mitigate the effects of global warming and Climate Change for this generation. It can only be reiterated that failure to do so shows a lack of professional conduct sufficient enough for the withdrawal of professional qualification to be mandatory.

Many innovative firms are developing a generation of new building materials. Materials are being engineered to be smarter, stronger, more self-sustaining, sleeker, and easier on the environment.

To keep a competitive edge, construction companies need to stay up-to-date on these materials and innovations. Buildings crafted with the most modern materials will be better equipped to solve the challenges.

While it can take decades for scientific breakthroughs to make their way to market, there are already lots available now.

Self-healing concrete, transparent aluminium, light-generating concrete, aluminium foam just boggle the mind. You would need to be a real enthusiast to know them all.

Invisible solar cells are used as windows. Solar is developing fast and competes on cost with wind power. It can come on stream to power thousands of homes in months not years.

Day by day the list grows. It is the mark of an organisation with a Royal Charter such as architects and surveyors that their members are aware of and implement these fast-evolving opportunities as a matter of professional practice.

Factory-built houses and units are able to use a wider range of materials.

Housing has not changed much in a generation. Gas, electricity, damp-proofing and a bit of insulation were being installed when Marty Quant popularised the mini skirt

In the face of global warming, unsustainable plunder of natural resources including concrete, brick and PVC are common and among the most environmentally damaging materials. They remain evident in hundreds of thousands of new houses built every year.

What should be an affordable, spacious refuge from Climate Change, a home office, the place for families to take advantage of the internet and Mixed Reality (a blend of physical and digital worlds, unlocking natural and intuitive 3D human, computer, and environmental interactions) and thrive for a generation is a great alternative.

We have learned that mono culture housing is socially difficult. Building a house complete or in modules in one or more factories is needed and already possible. Taking the modules to assemble on site for completion within a week is already commonly achieved but in niche applications.

Failure in delivering pre-built houses could be described by Greta Thunberg as "bla bla bla".

Contractors continue to say that architects and engineers are not adequately enabling prefabrication and/or modular construction in their design solutions.

Meanwhile, design professionals point to a shortage of prefabrication facilities close to their project sites and to owners' lack of understanding of the value of modular construction as the main reasons they do not design-in these approaches from the beginning of a project.

Design firms and contractors agree that significant improvements are available including cost, scheduling, quality, safety performance, productivity, client satisfaction and their ability to reduce waste.

There are many examples of prefabricated houses. Some are distressingly poorly designed and manufactured. Others are exemplars of modern design and meet very high standards.

Using more modern and environmentally friendly materials is necessary. Ramping up output from hundreds to thousands is not a big issue if the incentive and political leadership is there. These factory-built homes are not nearly as expensive to produce as the traditional mud-puddle-built competition. Furthermore, they can be built to equal the Passivehouse standards or better.

An example of this kind of thinking on a modest scale is an alliance of 29 housing associations and councils which have signed up six manufacturers to a new dynamic purchasing system to supply 2D panelised systems to be assembled on-site. The 2D systems suppliers list will run in parallel with the National Housing Federation's 'Building Better Framework'.

In factory-built houses many new additional options are possible. Solar, wind, rain and hot water harvesting can be optimised at minimal cost during manufacture. Such additions have a multiplier effect. In one house, the contribution is tiny in the national scheme of things but in 300,000 houses per year it is huge.

These issues and solutions are radical but significant opportunities for builders, the building industry and estate managers. Here we see a lower cost, faster delivery, competitive advantage, enhanced margins and a stable order book well into the future.

Prefabricated houses overcome problems of labour shortage, and reduce the time taken to complete. They make more money for the developer and there is a bonus for home buyers - factory made houses are cheaper.

The modern home can also be a refuge from the common cold, flu, Covid19, pollen, traffic pollutants and more. Why not save the NHS millions every year just by building better, virus-free, homes? Filtered air and heat exchange makes this possible. The health and social care costs of air pollution in England could reach £5.3 to 18.6 billion by 2035 (and was £157 million in 2017).

Homes can be built for communities that inter alia help to provide social care and reduce costs without asking the Chancellor for a bean.

The legacy of these and many more proposals will be felt for the life of the newly built houses lasting more than 50 years.

Often, the policy solutions cut across government department boundaries and between governments nationally and locally. These proposals do the same. In a housing crisis, some decisions need to override many impediments to success. Institutions that impede progress are both antisocial and economically damaging.

Modern designs have to address a range of interests.

The need for electrical energy over the next few decades is going to be huge. For the uses we have now, the ability to generate green energy when the wind drops in the winter and as gas supplies are disrupted by war in Ukraine, coal becomes king again and new oil wells in the North Sea spring to work.

Add to today's demand plus the fade out of gas for heating, cooking and hot water all has to be catered for. There is also demand for electric vehicles and even steel and concrete works.

Can our estates be used to generate green hydrogen to power big container ships and tonnes of this carbon-neutral fuel for air travel? There is an almost endless demand.

A new home that is not generating sufficient 'green' power for all the residents is obviously a failure in design and construction and an example of failure in modern construction and renewal. It also counts as a failure among the professionals.

Additionally, there will be a need for three-phase electricity to allow for fast car charging and other demands of a modern house.

The connection to the grid has to cease during a power cut to allow engineers to work on the grid without electrocuting themselves. This then is a role for the big estate batteries at the end of the street.

Many will be puzzled as to how green energy can be generated for a tower block.

It is not as hard as one might imagine. Big windows using solar power generating 'glass' and power generating cladding are obvious candidates and roofs are useful too (there is enough commercial roof area in the U.K. to generate around half of the country's electricity needs).

Vertical cladding for walls is useful for generating solar power and so too are canopies, curtain walls, facades, and skylight systems. Unlike traditional solar PV panels, cladding can be 'aesthetically appealing rather than a compromise to a building's design'. There is so much that can be done with solar energy creations.

Building-integrated photovoltaics (BIPV) are dual-purpose: they serve as both the outer layer of a structure and generate electricity for on-site use or export. In New York we can see interesting examples. The wall-mounted array performs equal to or better than the roof-mounted design for most of the autumn and winter. In the spring, production falls off moderately for the wall-mounted array and underperforms compared to the winter months.

In January in the UK a south-facing wall is more closely aligned to the sun's rays than a roof array.

In retrofit applications, vertical PV panels can also be used to camouflage unattractive or degraded building exteriors. Vertical cladding is also very useful for collecting heat throughout the year for hot water as well.

Standard building units have been used to deliver completely finished homes for decades and some of those homes are spectacular and still in daily use in upmarket neighbourhoods. These units range from complete homes to units that fit together to provide a much bigger residence.

When it comes to offsite construction, Britain is a 'laggard country'. That's the conclusion of Dale Steinhardt and Karen Manley of the Queensland University of Technology who compared offsite construction between several high-income countries. Less than 5% of construction in Britain uses offsite techniques, compared to around 9% in Germany, 12-15% in Japan and 20% in Sweden.

The Department for Business, Energy and Industrial Strategy response to the House of Lords Science and

164

Technology committee noted "There is an opportunity for the UK to maintain its position at the forefront (um... oh... OK) of off-site manufacture globally in the commercial and high-rise residential sectors. However, we are concerned that the UK lags significantly behind other countries in the low-rise residential sector.

Yet Britain has the largest factory devoted to modular construction in the world, owned by Legal and General and sited in Sherburn, Yorkshire. This company claims it has the capacity to build 3,000 new homes per year, showing off-site construction is not an alien concept to the British construction industry. Soon, a rival called Top Hat will produce a new house from its Leeds factory at the rate of a new house every hour.

Other modular units are designed with individual purpose in mind such as bathrooms, porches, kitchens, stairs etc.

Where repurposing takes place such units can be fitted in between buildings or can be added onto an existing building to enhance the quality of accommodation.

The advantages of this kind of thinking are myriad. Fully furnished rooms are already commonly factory fitted including kitchen lounge and dining furniture and much more. Such designs optimise space and are ready to move into.

Being standard modules, services such as electricity, air ducting and plumbing are standard and fit to a high engineering standard. Heat loss caused by thermal bridges (namely places where heat escapes) can be eliminated through good design and high specification manufacture. Installation of solar harvesting fitments including solar thermal panels on roofs and walls collect heat for water. It is a simple add-on in a factory built house and a pain for builders clambering over roofs in a howling gale.

The speed of manufacture is another bonus. Design is, for the most part, standard but some sites and some specifiers may require tweaks. This is a digital process which takes days and costs little.

Computerised design and manufacture is a process almost from start to finish. It reduces the development and production time compared to the traditional mud puddle housing estate.

Prefab homes up to five storeys high are not unknown and 2D tower block construction has already been used.

Designing factory-produced elements (using computer-aided design software) is helpful in renovating existing buildings and the conversion of shops, offices warehouses and factories into homes.

Delivery within three weeks is common and depends only on completed site groundworks for the dwelling to be ready for occupation.

Now, the opportunities are evident and the threats are obvious.

Issues of labour shortage and upstream supply shortage are discussed in a later chapter but one thing is clear: the need to resolve delay has to be dealt with.

The piecemeal approach to solving issues like the range of insulation quality along a street may be resolved in the eventual demolition of some dwellings to bring the street up to standard.

Construction has to change and the ability to do it is not a distant dream.

The political chatter and civil service obfuscation across the many associated departments of government is a muddle to behold. It is time that politicians were better-informed and that government was to shed its bureaucratic walls; the designers and architects changed the habits of centuries and the manufacturers tooled up.

Sources and References

"Building-Integrated Photovoltaics | SEIA." Solar Energy Industries Association, https://www.seia.org/initiatives/building-integrated-photovoltaics. Accessed 19 April 2022.

Carmona, Matthew. "80. Women and the scourge of fearful streets." Matthew Carmona, 16 March 2021, https://matthew-carmona.com/2021/03/16/women-and-the-scourge-of-fearful-streets/. Accessed 19 April 2022.

Chen, Feihu, et al. "Energy and Built Environment - Journals." KeAi Publishing, http://www.keaipublishing.com/en/journals/energy-and-built-envir onment/. Accessed 19 April 2022.

Clover, Ian. "UK solar leaders launch comprehensive commercial rooftop PV guide." PV Magazine, 20 July 2016, https://www.pv-magazine.com/2016/07/20/uk-solar-leaders-launch-comprehensive-commercial-rooftop-pv-guide_100025495/. Accessed 19 April 2022.

"18 Future Building Materials That Will Change Construction." BigRentz, 4 December 2018, https://www.bigrentz.com/blog/the-future-of-building-materials. Accessed 19 April 2022.

"Exploring Modular Homes - Cheapest Path to Net Zero?"

YouTube, 29 June 2021,

https://www.youtube.com/watch?v=tOy1rk8QHt4.

Accessed 19

April 2022.

"5 Disadvantages of Vertical Axis Wind Turbine (VAWT) | The Windy Blog." LuvSide, 31 March 2020, https://www.luvside.de/en/vawt-disadvantages/. Accessed 19 April 2022.

Gibson, Scott. "Balanced Whole-House Ventilation - GreenBuildingAdvisor." Green Building Advisor, 8 October 2021,

https://www.greenbuildingadvisor.com/article/balanced-whole-hou se-ventilation. Accessed 19 April 2022.

Haroldson, Canute. "Wall-mounted solar: A rising trend or barely hanging on?" Solar Power World, 31 July 2017, https://www.solarpowerworldonline.com/2017/07/wall-mounted-so lar-trend/. Accessed 19 April 2022.

"Incorporating solar harvesting into the side of buildings could enhance energy sustainability: Research demonstrates the potential of a solar unit that can hang on the outside of a structure." ScienceDaily, 5 August 2020, https://www.sciencedaily.com/releases/2020/08/200805110 130.ht

m.   Accessed 19 April 2022.

"Latest figures show increase in new energy efficient homes."

GOV.UK, 29 July 2021,

https://www.gov.uk/government/news/latest-figures-show-increase-in-new-energy-efficient-homes. Accessed 19 April 2022.

Limb, Lottie. "Solar panels built from waste crops can make energy without direct light." Euronews, 26 February 2022,

https://www.euronews.com/green/2022/02/19/solar-panels-built-fr om-waste-crops-can-make-energy-without-direct-light.   Accessed 19 April 2022.

Miles, David. "Constraints to offsite construction in the UK." Atamate,

https://www.atamate.com/atamate-blog/constraints-to-offsite-const ruction-in-britain. Accessed 19 April 2022.

"Modular   Range."   Beattie Passive,
https://beattiepassive.com/modular.php. Accessed 19 April 2022.

"New tool calculates NHS and social care costs of air pollution."

GOV.UK, 22 May 2018,

https://www.gov.uk/government/news/new-tool-calculates-nhs-and-social-care-costs-of-air-pollution.Accessed 19 April 2022.

"Prefabrication and Modular Construction 2020 | Dodge Data & Analytics." Dodge Data and Analytics, https://www.construction.com/toolkit/reports/prefabrication-modul ar-construction-2020. Accessed 19 April 2022.

Randall, Ian. "Neanderthals cleared a forest in Germany 125000 years ago." Daily Mail, 16 December 2021, https://www.dailymail.co.uk/sciencetech/article-10316207/Archae ology-Neanderthals-cleared-forest-Germany-fire-tools-125-000-years-ago.html. Accessed 14 April 2022.

"Recent progress of efficient flexible solar cells based on nanostructures." Journal of Semiconductors, http://www.jos.ac.cn/article/id/3ed0e42d-0632-4830-8b47-4f09f1a 2780a?viewType=HTML. Accessed 19 April 2022.

Simmons, Dan. "DIY energy: UK solar inventions could reduce bills." BBC, 1 April 2022, https://www.bbc.com/news/technology-60922527. Accessed 19 April 2022.

Spyro, Steph. "Public concern on green issues at highest level, poll finds." Daily Express, 10 November 2021, https://www.express.co.uk/news/nature/1519431/cop26-green-issu es-public-concern-highest-level-poll. Accessed 19 April 2022.

"A Tour of Factory-Built Houses | This Old House." YouTube, 10 March 2021, https://www.youtube.com/watch?v=MWrw_bSjHA8. Accessed 19 April 2022.

Wilson, James. "The Potential of Prefab: How Modular Construction Can Be Green." BuildingGreen, 9 September 2019, https://www.buildinggreen.com/feature/potential-prefab-how-mod ular-construction-can-be-green. Accessed 19 April 2022.

Chapter 8: Breathing New Life Into Houses

Types of dwelling

There are probably 28 million homes in the UK that urgently need renovation, insulation and improvement. Past schemes offered by the Government have not worked but some initiatives have been successful. Perhaps it is time to examine the work that has to be done against the background of Climate Change, housing shortage and evolving technologies.

Without a doubt, the work of 'The London Energy Transformation Initiative' (LETI) is useful and provides retrofit examples.

There is a great range of dwellings we may want to look at, and they can be examined in this list:

Tower blocks

Converted offices, warehouses and others Multistorey dwellings

Low rise

Detached/ semi and terraced houses

Back to back

Singlestorey bungalows and chalets

Holiday chalets and residential park homes etc,

It will require some imagination to propose solutions for such a wide range of homes. Perhaps that is the essential consideration, working on providing homes, not simply dwellings.

The planning process outlined in chapter 7 still needs to apply in renovation, repurposing and rebuilding. After careful research homes need to be built to suit local needs. Posh repurposed dwellings with homeless beggars at the front door and elderly relatives stuffed into a bedroom are no solution.

Time to think BIG. We will need more space to live indoors. If it is too hot to go out then space to live in is critical.

There is also a mindset among those who would rebuild and refurbish houses and estates to create a gentrified model. The 'renovated/rebuilt Garden City districts of mixed dwellings designed for middle class residents, students and the retired with lots of gardens filled with poplar and willow saplings on green space lawns is faulty. It seems that various neighbourhood habits become at odds with each other as a result of introducing new residents. Particularly low income residents feel their ways of life are becoming threatened. In terms of the right to the city debate, it is important to ask the question as to how democratic the mixing process is as well as how daily neighbourhood rhythms and perceptions of neighbourhood space are affected. The disadvantaged, by their nature, are not well represented in the debate about what rebuilding means to them.

The use of socioeconomic analysis of local communities to identify a real need at a point in time is essential.

It is evident that some standards need to be adhered to. Homes need to be well insulated and warm in winter and cool in summer. Not damp but dry with clean filtered air. The accommodation has to be adequate for current and future generations of users and set in a wellmanaged estate. Pokey flatlets in exoffice blocks rightly have a poor reputation. As we continue to evolve, it is the case that homes will continue to grow in size.

Essentials in breathing new life

Using modern techniques and technologies it is still important to harvest energy and all the naysayers who can't understand that a north facing wall can yield/store power now have to examine the fast developing science and evolving products. Additionally, there are a number of combined electricity and heat harvesting capabilities now available.

Normally it takes a long time to bring science to the consumer but we have discovered from the Covid pandemic that it can be done in weeks not years. If for the Covid emergency, then so too for the housing crisis. It is a matter of will and may need Government support and impetus.

But, preferably, not money.

While a high proportion of urban homes are in dire need of being refurbished, it is important to think of those in the countryside as well.

Quaint old farmhouses are renowned for being draughty and difficult to heat.

It is not only the cost of homes that is an issue, the ability to implement environmental and renovation enhancement also has to face problems of ownership and finance.

The range of properties that have to be considered is extensive and this chapter deals with the most obvious.

Tenements, back to backs, highrise blocks of flats and office conversions appear alongside postwar bungalows, three bed semi detached suburbs and their swankier 'desirable detached houses with double garage'.

Ownership ranges from commercial residential property investors seeking a return on the conversion of an office block to flats and the single, mortgaged, homeowner.

Already, the relaxed British planning regime has produced some horrid designs and pokey damp flats in iffy neighbourhoods. Homes over, say, 30 years old offer opportunities for modernisation. But, such repurposed homes need to be equipped to survive the effects of Climate

Change and evolving lifestyles and changes. The Cambridge Carbon Footprint project is informative and offers some good case studies of refurbishment required to make existing houses Climate Change ready.

Some dwellings are in the hands of greedy landlords attempting to cram as many people into a single, poorly managed building; others are in respectable postwar housing boom estates. Inevitably, the aim of creating well planned, spacious and comfortable, environmentally neutral or better homes is a challenge.

The age of some designs go back to about 1706 and Glaswegians still live in tenements that were first built in the 1860s.

Once again recourse to long term commercial money is key. A guaranteed return on a stable asset is needed. The long suffering taxpayer should not be penalised for lack of housing maintenance and repurposing.

In looking at the problem, the issue of what we need in our dwellings has to be ready for days when the outside temperature is beyond 35 centigrade during frequent heatwaves. There is also wintertime highpressure weather. This bringing low wind speeds and stationary windmills. And then, of course, comes the occasional bonechilling 'Beast from the East'.

This prompts us to think of housing families including children and aged parents in the same home and for at least one family member working from home. The need to mitigate the effects of Global Warming generated Climate Change and to work even further in reducing carbon emissions (especially if countries like China are not making their contribution) is essential.

Additionally, there are going to be some big new demands to be fulfilled. Hydrogen to power ships and trucks and planes, yet more electricity and hydrogen to make more steel, glass and cement and top up electric cars.

How much will it cost

Working from the Construction Leadership Council figures, the average cost of upgrading all the homes that need it in the UK will cost about £18,714 each (some say more) and will take until 2040.

The present Government policy is nibbling away at doing the right thing.

Tiny sums of money are being spread around and managed by people checking on who is eligible and then dishing out taxpayers' money. Of course, the cost of all these people involved is just more money wasted because there is no coherent policy but plenty of regulations. Monitoring the quality of workmanship is at best variable. There is a case for registering quality assured vendors and tradespeople using professional institutions and blockchain management to provide cheap and immutable audits.

There are many things that are essential to cope with Climate Change.

The Government has a fixation on solving the global warming target set by COP26.

HMG proposes "a longterm strategy that would refurbish all of the UK's homes by 2040. This would cost £524bn in total, it says, of which the Government would need to invest £168bn, and would create 500,000 jobs". But £600 per home is just not enough.

Assuming that this amount of money is spent actually on upgrading homes and not on advisors or government employees, this will be a useful amount of money. It will require a number of partners including private funding, local authority input in the delivery of local housing needs, surveys, planning consent and developers. Delivered estate wide it will be of value. But not of much value if at its core is the laying of bricks.

Perovskite photovoltaic windows, which go from being transparent to opaque on heatwave days and which convert absorbed sunlight into electricity, are a promising green technology which contributes to the principle of a dwelling that generates income for the homeowner.

But, there are other opportunities for saved costs in the refurbishment of homes. The NHS spends at least £2.5 billion a year treating people with illnesses directly linked to living in cold, damp and dangerous conditions.

In 2020, the costs of air pollution to the NHS and social care in England were estimated to be £157 million. The latest findings, published in a report from Public Health England, warn these costs could reach £18.6 billion by 2035 unless action is taken.

If these sums of money are not needed for the NHS they can be diverted for the renovation of UK housing. It is a tough decision but has to be done. There is no reason why the NHS should not sponsor the installation of air filters in all the houses of an estate. The return on such an investment for the NHS would be swift.

Enhanced accommodation for the elderly living within the family will be a significant saving in Social Care budgets as well.

The provision of wide corridors, housing for mobility scooters, spacious and disabled mitigation design, wet rooms and care facilities in the home will cut down on carer costs and help families look after the growing elderly population.

Ownership

Who owns these ailing properties? There are so many people involved in ownership. And they vary depending on the types of dwellings including empty, unused dwellings (9% of the housing stock).

A proportion of homes are owned by the occupier, more are part owned against a loan such as a parent, a coowner, building society, bank, or a range of other money lenders. There are a lot of other organisations and people who have a lean over properties where owners have used the properties as security. Lease and rent are common forms of holding.

The highrise and tenement estates also have complex ownerships. Many estates are owned as commercial investments with their shareholders as the eventual landlords.

There are, as we have seen, many other stakeholders with an interest.

They seek to develop their property including farmers, warehouse and office owners. Residential properties above shops (frequently in rundown High Streets). It can be complicated and needs strong people to make some sense of it all and repurpose buildings to a high Climate Change mitigation standard.

It is not often that a physical bulldozer is a solution.

There are many other parties with an interest in 'citizen groups'. These stakeholders range from the utilities to schools. Their involvement can be helpful. They often have a physical presence and an investment (like the NHS above).

The value of their presence and investment is part 'owned' by local dwelling occupiers. This is a joint asset and as such has a value which can be used to assist the funding for The Estate development and revival.

What to do with empty houses?

Help is at hand. The What Works Centre for Local Economic Growth is jointly run by the LSE and Centre for Cities and funded by the Economic and Social Research Council, the Department for Business Energy and Industrial Strategy, the Department for Levelling Up, Housing and Communities, and the Department for Transport.

Its activities include reviewing and highlighting the evidence on what local economic policy works and it shapes a framework that runs alongside the ideas in this book.

In essence, it examines the areas most in need of renewal.

The Centre is not as focussed on achieving big change at no cost to the public purse as can be found here and, as can be seen by the range funders, has to stumble over the rubble of government departments to achieve its purpose.

Beyond Global Warming

Global Warming is a big issue but it is Climate Change that forces us to examine the several fundamentals that could or, alternatively, should be considered for all new builds, redevelopment of run down areas or repurposing buildings.

There is a problem with attempting to recommend particular solutions or technologies because they change fast.

That is not to say that this is an excuse to wait. Implementation should have begun yesterday as indeed, to a limited extent, it did.

The big push at present is to double glaze, insulate, eliminate heat bridges, replace gas heating and add heat pumps. Yes, all good. It should save money for the residents, keep them warm and reduce mouldy walls.

Solar energy from the whole roof is a no brainer. Half a dozen black patches on a roof is just not sensible. They look like Deadeye Dick's decaying teeth. Energy from light and heat harvesting has to be a big part of building renovation as for new builds. The capability of a roof to bear the weight of solar cells is no longer an issue. Some solar cells are millimetres thick and quite flexible.

Then there is wind harvesting using windmills; including vertical windmills that can even be fitted to a normal detached house.

But now we come to wall cladding that generates electricity and also provides hot water all year round.

The refurbishment of highrise flats with new cladding, insulation and fireproofing tall buildings after the Grenfell disaster is a case in point. The revenues from installing solar harvesting walls would go a long way to financing this effort. In addition harvesting power from windows (with air filtering a big bonus for the NHS) and vertical windmills installed from top to bottom would also help. It seems that the time to have 'thinking' windows is upon us. Afterall dualpane windows were invented back in 1865. So in 1870, they were truly best of class but now we can have windows that do not let heat in or out and can also harvest solar heat and electricity. This suggests that bigger windows have many useful and immediate benefits. The regulators in London think smaller windows are a better solution! Making the cladding and windows of a highrise into a value creator instead of a cost is a no-brainer. At the same time building an estate wide 5G mesh wifi will be fun for every teenager in their bedrooms and mum and dad as well. It's better than broadband.

As the Internet of Things (IoT) becomes more common, estate wide wifi will be a big help. Is this how the grass will be cut, bins emptied, roads swept, public toilets cleaned, and windows washed? Of course, it will. Automation will happen and much faster than most imagine.

Automated garden irrigation (with weather forecasting and soil moisture sensors) is already here.

This is an appeal to Governments to put as much effort into developing solar power as for covid vaccination. The emergence of graphene based solar harvesting materials sounds exciting. Filtered air to keep people healthy and reduce passing on Covid, flu and colds as well as keeping pollen count and road pollution from children, the old and mum and dad is very important. Window blinds that harvest solar energy can also power air filtration and seems quite sensible, especially in highrise buildings.

The use of plastics in the revival of old houses is not a good idea. Plastic is on its way to outpacing coal plants in terms of greenhouse gas emissions. In fact, plastic could have a larger carbon footprint than coal by the end of the decade.

Balcony gardens and small backyards can be developed into attractive, carbon capturing and productive green spaces. There are many advantages in having small gardens where space is at a premium. From purer air to mental health the benefits are useful for city dwellers.

Transportable, instant balconies can add a lot to a house or tenement.

They can be used for solarpowered minigreenhouses (some are even designed for highrise balconies). Vertical flower and vegetable hydroponic gardens and garden beds are already being sold.

One can also hear the rumble of demolition. The use of land for new and extended (factory built) homes is one thought but some of this space can be used for parking to remove all those cars half parked on pavements. Battery charging, car share and other benefits can be helpful in generating estate revenues (not, of course, forgetting wind and solar power collected from street lights, bus shelters and bike racks etc.).

Whatever is done to revive and renovate the majority of UK dwellings there are two elephants in the room: manpower and supplies.

Finding trained and educated manpower is going to be difficult. There is already a government endorsed scheme to register adequate services called Trustmark. This is a scheme to weed out 'Bodgit and Sons', the fly by night insulation firms. This issue is so bad that the government has entered the fray with guidance for householders. The builder's chartered institution (COIB) should now solve the problem. Then we can shoo away the government and Treasury.

Energy Company Obligation (ECO) is a Government energy efficiency scheme in Great Britain to help reduce carbon emissions and tackle fuel poverty. Ofgem administers the scheme on behalf of the Department for Energy, Business & Industrial Strategy. Its duties include:

- allocating a proportion of targets to obligated suppliers
- monitoring supplier progress and deciding whether they've achieved their obligations
- reporting to the Secretary of State

- auditing, ensuring compliance and preventing and detecting fraud.

Cutting through this jungle of bureaucratic jobs for the boys needs attention.

Ofgem says it delivers renewable energy and social programmes on behalf of the government. "Our expertise lies in designing, setting up and delivering largescale programmes in the sustainable energy sector. These programmes are in fields as diverse as renewable heat, renewable electricity, energy efficiency and fuel poverty."

The auditing of the countryside covered in solar panels; huge windmills from horizon to horizon off the coast and battery farms as big as Manchester airport is, no doubt, important. It is possibly it could be a blockchain programme that sits on a computer in the government Minister's First Secretary's desk. It should, of course, be monitored and policed by the Chartered Insitute of Purchasing and Supply and comes under the same rules that apply to all Chartered Institutes identified in this book and thereby costs the taxpayer next to nothing.

Moving energy production to households and electricity power balancing to estates (old and new) will remove much of the need for ECO.

In 2021 Bridgend County Borough Council found it may have to pay over £1 million to repair 100 new homes that were fitted with poor insulation. It gives the impression that there are a lot of government departments spending time and taxpayers' money to offer ever more information and schemes? Could a lot of this waste be used at the sharp end? Can the COIB be dragooned into doing its job?

Training, qualifications and a professional institution with real powers are needed. Examples such as the Chartered Institute of Building have to come to the party. Of course, once again we should expect such an institution to monitor the quality of members' work and be responsible for maintaining only excellent members. At that point, the cost of training and supervision currently paid for by the Government vanishes and the money is diverted to renovation etc. Such an institute might also be responsible for the recruitment of people into the building profession and maintaining the level of technical innovation across the membership (and in particular the use and application of factory built houses and modules).

The issue of tradespeople getting old is worth considering. Building work is, in many cases, hard manual labour and ageing workers can find it difficult. It is also the case that heat, cold and rain often make this work unattractive. At the same time, the number of younger people coming into the sector is quite low. Labour is short. Adding to this is the number of self employed in the construction sector. It is more common than any other. Wage Cost inflation is high too. There are new capabilities being developed all the time including automation.

These factors limit the availability of craftspeople in the sector. Some activities are being automated which will help.

There is some light at the end of the tunnel. Prefabricated buildings are built indoors and work is supported by a wide range of technologies and automation that take the hard graft out of construction.

For some time shortages of materials have been an issue. It seems as though the construction sector and their upstream suppliers have not understood what the word 'crisis' really means.

At the end of 2021, 82% of builders had delayed jobs due to a lack of materials, while 60% pressed pause on a job due to a lack of tradespeople. An industry survey revealed that the quantities of general labourers, carpenters/joiners and plasterers were all down by 6% over a month.

All those houses, all that renovation and rebuilding to be done and there is a shortage of supplies. Perhaps it is because some builders have only just cottoned on. They still don't understand, for example, that solar panel sun and wind shades over balconies will protect their customers from the heat and can be constructed to mitigate the impact of sudden, unexpected violent storms. Their world is different. It needs forward looking and urgent and comprehensive action.

It's coming. It's part of the new building paradigm.

British Steel blamed 2022 new year steelmaking costs for a further hike of steel prices, prompting exasperation from contractors. The price of steel rose by £50 a tonne, the company said in a letter to contractors across the UK. British Steel blamed the sustained high level of steelmaking cost.

The construction materials shortage was easing, but long lead times and further price increases for some products were expected. How the industry ran short of bricks and tiles in the middle of a housing CRISIS is simply silly. The vendor chain could be aware of the housing crisis (and the old-fashioned need for bricks) and so could the Government and its bloated civil service.

Yet, once again, the bureaucracy got in the way of policy.

If, when all renovated and rebuilt homes of any scale have to undertake the same analysis as for new housing estates it will prove need versus speculation and mandate time scale. It will not be long because the housing needs change and so there will have to be a time limit on how long it will take to complete and hand over the properties.

There already is a potential capability in the rules for planning. The local 'Development Plan' invites local authorities to set the rules and one of those rules can include details of timescales for the completion of projects.

Implementing the new build, refurbishing, repurposing and renewal of practically the whole housing stock is a daunting thought. However, we know that over the next couple of decades this is what we have to achieve starting now in every street and estate. It also means there is a need for government and the various commercial sectors to understand that this is the imperative that has to met.

A lot of this action is down to finance which is dealt with below.

For new builds, the plan is reasonably clear. The process is to build homes against local need and not speculatively. The margins would be less, speed of (factory) build would be much faster and the added facility of the homes would cost less with added factory quality assured production.

Refurbishing homes is a matter of degree. At present an extra layer of insulation, taping up heat bridges, replacing the gas boiler and fitting a heat exchanger seems to be the basic deal.

Here is a 'cosy' home saving pennies on heating and reducing CO_2 emissions. Its helpful but not really preparing for Climate Change. There is a standard that applies to refurbishing older properties called EnerPHit (a house renovation capability in the Passive House activity) which is a good basis for helping deal with Climate Change.

It sets out a series of standards that offer a good basis for the renovation of houses.

The nation knows that there is a huge problem and so it is time to act.

Sources and References

Cambridge CarbonFootprint: Home, https://cambridgecarbonfootprint.org/. Accessed 21 April 2022.

Renewable energy solutions Off grid energy storage,

http://www.solarconstructions.com/. Accessed 22 April 2022.

Plasma Kinetics, https://plasmakinetics.com/. Accessed 24 April 2022.

Toilitech: Selfcleaning toilets and public toilets solutions, https://www.toilitech.com/. Accessed 25 April 2022.

TrustMark Government Endorsed Scheme For Work Done Around Your Home, https://www.trustmark.org.uk/. Accessed 25 April 2022.

CIOB Home Page | CIOB, https://www.ciob.org/. Accessed 25 April 2022.

Chandler, David L. "New approach suggests path to emissionsfree cement." MIT News, 16 September 2019, https://news.mit.edu/2019/carbondioxideemissionsfreecement0916. Accessed 25 April 2022.

"Climate Emergency Retrofit Guide." LETI, 21 October 2021,

https://www.leti.london/retrofit. Accessed 21 April 2022.

"Combining Heat Pumps And Solar Panel Heating (2022)." GreenMatch, https://www.greenmatch.co.uk/blog/2015/07/combininghea tpumps andsolarpanelheating. Accessed 24 April 2022.

"COP26 Goals UN Climate Change Conference." COP26, https://ukcop26.org/cop26goals/. Accessed 25 April 2022.

"The cost of unhealthy housing to the NHS, House of Commons, 26 February 2019." Local Government Association, 26 February 2019, https://www.local.gov.uk/parliament/briefingsandresponses /costun healthyhousingnhshousecommons26february2019. Accessed 25 April 2022.

Crist, Ry. "Starlink Explained: Ething to Know About Elon Musk's Satellite Internet Venture." CNET, 25 April 2022, https://www.cnet.com/home/internet/starlinksatelliteinterne texplain ed/. Accessed 30 April 2022.

Deign, Jason. "Germany's MaxedOut Grid Is Causing Trouble Across Europe." Greentech Media, 31 March 2020, https://www.greentechmedia.com/articles/read/germanysstr essedgr idiscausingtroubleacrosseurope. Accessed 30 April 2022.

Demaitre, Eugene. "Trombia Free autonomous street sweeper launched by Finnish startup." The Robot Report, 29 September 2020,

https://www.therobotreport.com/trombiafreeautonomousstr eetswee perlaunched/. Accessed 25 April 2022.

"DIY 1960s EnerPHit retrofit." YouTube, 21 October 2021, https://www.youtube.com/watch?v=OVcvk9Wnyw4. Accessed 30 April 2022.

"Ecosystembased adaptation to Climate Change through residential urban green structures: cobenefits to thermal comfort, biodiversity, carbon storage and social interaction." One Ecosystem, 16 December 2021, https://oneecosystem.pensoft.net/article/65706/.

Accessed 25 April 2022.

"Energy Company Obligation (ECO)." Ofgem, https://www.ofgem.gov.uk/environmentalandsocialschemes /energy companyobligationeco. Accessed 25 April 2022.

"Energy Efficiency of Existing Homes Environmental Audit Committee House of Commons." Energy Efficiency of Existing Homes Environmental Audit Committee House of Commons, 22 March 2021,

https://publications.parliament.uk/pa/cm5801/cmselect/cme nvaud/ 346/34605.htm. Accessed 25 April 2022.

"Estimation of costs to the NHS and social care due to the health impacts of air pollution: summary report." GOV.UK, https://assets.publishing.service.gov.uk/government/upload s/system/uploads/attachment_data/file/708855/Estimation_ of_costs_to_the_NHS_and_social_care_due_to_the_health _impacts_of_air_pollu tion summary_report.pdf. Accessed 25 April 2022.

"Falkirk confirms £347m housing spend." Construction Index, 20 January 2022, https://www.theconstructionindex.co.uk/news/view/falkirkc onfirm s347mhousingspend. Accessed 21 April 2022.

"Find energy grants and ways to save energy in your home." GOV.UK, https://www.gov.uk/improveenergyefficiency. Accessed 21 April 2022.

"5 Best Smart Robotic Window Cleaners In 2020." YouTube, 3 February 2020, https://www.youtube.com/watch?v=zMSXx7TgguE. Accessed 25 April 2022.

Harvey, Fiona. "Retrofitting leaky homes would cost £5bn over next four years, UK ministers told." The Guardian, 28 May 2021,

https://www.theguardian.com/environment/2021/may/28/re
trofittin

gleakyhomeswouldcost5bnovernextfouryearsukministerstol
d. Accessed 21 April 2022.

Herring, Chris. "Retrofitting to Passive House standards."

YouTube, 14 March 2021,

https://www.youtube.com/watch?v=wN34zF7e4J8.

Accessed 30

April 2022.

Hewitt, Daniel. "Investigation launched into 'disgusting' damp and mouldy council housing." ITV, 13 April 2021,

https://www.itv.com/news/20210413/investigationlaunched
intodisg

ustingdampandmouldycouncilhousingafteritvnewsreport.
Accessed 21 April 2022.

"Home energy grants — Simple Energy Advice." Simple Energy Advice,

https://www.simpleenergyadvice.org.uk/grants. Accessed 21 April 2022.

"House Renovation Cost in 2022." Checkatrade,

https://www.checkatrade.com/blog/costguides/costrenovati
nghouse

/. Accessed 25 April 2022.

"ITM Power gears up for green hydrogen revolution." The Engineer, 7 March 2022, https://www.theengineer.co.uk/itmpowergearsupforgreenhydrogenr evolution/. Accessed 30 April 2022.

"Jo Wheeler: Local authorities can drive a home retrofit revolution." Local Government Chronicle, 4 August 2021, https://www.lgcplus.com/politics/climatechange/jowheelerl ocalaut horitiescandriveahomeretrofitrevolution04082021/. Accessed 25

April 2022.

Keller, Michael. "Growing carbon footprint for plastics."

ScienceDaily, 2 December 2021, https://www.sciencedaily.com/releases/2021/12/211202113 504.htm. Accessed 25 April 2022.

Lang, Alan. "Hydrogen storage for residential homes: new solutions for a new idea." GKN, 12 May 2018, https://news.pminnovationblog.com/blog/hydrogenstoragef orreside ntialhomesnewsolutionsforan ewidea. Accessed 24 April 2022.

Lodder, Doug. "Broadband in the 5G Era: Why Multifamily Housing Properties are Adopting Communitywide Networks." Broadband Communities,

https://www.bbcmag.com/multifamilybroadband/broadban
dinthe5g
erawhymultifamilyhousingpropertiesareadoptingcommunit
ywidene tworks. Accessed 25 April 2022.

Ly, Chen. "Smart windows keep heat in during winter and
let it out in summer." New Scientist, 16 December 2021,
https://www.newscientist.com/article/2302249smartwindo
wskeeph eatinduringwinterandletitoutinsummer/. Accessed
25 April 2022.

Major's, John. "UK urban regeneration initiative fails to
help those in deprived areas | LSE Research." London
School of Economics,
https://www.lse.ac.uk/research/researchfortheworld/politics
/govern
menturbanregenerationinitiativefailedtoimprovebritainsmos
tdepriv edareas. Accessed 21 April 2022.

Matheson, Jim. "Glasgow Tenements." SGHET, 20 May
2020,
https://sghet.com/tenements/. Accessed 22 April 2022.

"Meeting housing demand London." UK Parliament
Committees,
10 January 2022,
https://committees.parliament.uk/publications/8354/docum
ents/852 92/default/. Accessed 21 April 2022.

Mitchell, Andy. "Greening Our Existing Homes." Construction Leadership Council, https://www.constructionleadershipcouncil.co.uk/wpconten t/uploa ds/2021/05/ConstructionLeade rshipCouncilNationalRetrofitStrategyVersion2.pdf.Accessd 21 April 2022.

"Passivhaus Retrofit introduction." Passivhaus Trust, https://www.passivhaustrust.org.uk/competitions_and_cam paigns/p assivhausretrofit/. Accessed 30 April 2022.

"[PDF] IOT Based Grass Cutter Using Solar Energy." Semantic Scholar, https://www.semanticscholar.org/paper/IOTBasedGrassCut terUsin gSolarEnergyNivedithaBhuva neshwari/d37b96a80fe960d575dac4cda210745678380bdd. Accessed 25 April 2022.

Peplow, Mark. "Can industry decarbonize steelmaking?" C&EN, 13 June 2021, https://cen.acs.org/environment/greenchemistry/steelhydrog enlowc o2startups/99/i22. Accessed 23 April 2022.

"Retrofit for the Future – BRE Trust." BRE Trust, 10 August 2020, https://www.bretrust.org.uk/knowledgehub/retrofitforthefut ure/. Accessed 25 April 2022.

Rodrigues, Caroline. "Enerphit: the Passivhaus retrofit method Grand Designs magazine." Grand Designs Magazine,

https://www.granddesignsmagazine.com/renovate/extend/enerphitp assivhausretrofit/. Accessed 30 April 2022.

Stein, Joshua. "Material shortages: bricks and roof tiles still in short supply." Construction News, 19 January 2022,

https://www.constructionnews.co.uk/supplychain/materials hortage sbricksandrooftilesstillinshorts

upply19012022/. Accessed 30 April 2022.

Sweetser, Robin. "10 Things to Consider When Balcony Gardening." The Old Farmer's Almanac,

https://www.almanac.com/10tipsstartingbalconygarden. Accessed 25 April 2022.

"Toward smart net zero energy structures: Development of cementbased structural energy material for contact electrification driven energy harvesting and storage." Kyung Hee University, 23 November 2021,

https://khu.elsevierpure.com/en/publications/towardsmartne tzeroen ergystructuresdevelopmentofcementbas. Accessed 23 April 2022.

"UK monthly property transactions commentary." GOV.UK, 21 April 2022,

https://www.gov.uk/government/statistics/monthlypropertyt ransacti onscompletedintheukwithvalu40000orabove/ukmonthlypro pertytra nsactionscommentary. Accessed 25 April 2022.

"What is a ventilated facade and why should you use it for your building?" Rockpanel, 1 June 2020, https://www.rockpanel.co.uk/inspiration/infocentre/whatisa ventilat edfacadeandwhyshouldyouuseitforyourbuilding/. Accessed 25 April 2022.

Williams, Fran, and Rob Wilson. "RetroFirst – A campaign by The Architects' Journal." The Architects' Journal, https://www.architectsjournal.co.uk/news/retrofirst. Accessed 21 April 2022.

Woodfield, Jack. "Spring Statement 2022: VAT Cut on EnergySaving Home Improvements." Homebuilding & Renovating, 23 March 2022, https://www.homebuilding.co.uk/news/springstatementann ouncem ents. Accessed 21 April 2022.

"Work begins on £11.7m Queens Gardens redevelopment." Hull CC News, 14 February 2022, https://www.hullccnews.co.uk/14/02/2022/workbeginson11 7mquee nsgardensredevelopment/. Accessed 21 April 2022.

Major's, John. "UK urban regeneration initiative fails to help those in deprived areas | LSE Research." London School of Economics,

https://www.lse.ac.uk/research/researchfortheworld/politics/govern

menturbanregenerationinitiativefailedtoimprovebritainsmostdepriv edareas. Accessed 17 May 2022.

"Why estate renewal?" What Works Centre for Local Economic Growth, https://whatworksgrowth.org/policyreviews/estaterenewal/ whyesta terenewal/. Accessed 17 May 2022.

Chapter 9: Time and Money

Money! It's the hard thing to consider in this book.

One of the key players in this subject area is the Green Finance Institute. Its objectives are: "To achieve the transition to an inclusive, net zero carbon and climate resilient economy, both public and private finance is needed."

In an interesting press release in November 2021 it announced a new initiative:

"The need to unlock finance to retrofit homes in the owner occupier sector is now clearly recognised, and the range of products available is beginning to grow, with pioneering financial institutions launching and continually developing new ways of lending for energy efficiency upgrades."

The idea of such an organisation is worthy. However, most of its thinking is focused on mitigating global warming and not Climate Change.

It is an example of the confused thinking among those that have come to global warming and its impacts late.

There are other such worthy organisations. ESG – short for Environmental, Social and Governance – is a set of standards measuring a business's impact on society, the environment, and how transparent and accountable it is.

According to the CBI, two thirds of investors take ESG factors into account when investing in a company meaning ESG has the potential to grow a business while benefiting the environment and community.

More than 10 mortgage lenders in the UK have launched green mortgage products since the beginning of 2021 alone, but this is a relatively small proportion of the UK's £1.58 trillion mortgage market. According to the Intermediary Mortgage Lenders Association, 77% of lenders are planning to launch green mortgages that are cheaper or priced the same as a typical product. Acting as a central knowledge hub, the Green Finance Institute has launched the Green Mortgage Hub, an online resource collating publicly available information on UK green mortgages into an interactive table, alongside a library of articles, reports, tools and experiments related to the green mortgage market. The hub aims to inform and encourage lenders considering entry into the green mortgage market. It aims to be a trusted source of information for mortgage intermediaries, policymakers and NGOs focused on decarbonising the built environment (that is global warming mitigation but not necessarily Climate Change) management.

The Green Mortgage Hub has a list of lenders offering a range of services. However, there is the other side of the coin. The current forms of finance are a form of tax and it is difficult for a large proportion of the population.

There is a need to get monthly housing payments down to no more than 25% or 30% of the principal wage earner's income.

At the same time we need to invest in both new houses, renewal and refurbishment of the existing housing stock (to meet global warming and Climate Change targets) which is the raison d'etre for Green Finance Institute. But it has to be combined with many other financial players.

Already we have looked at how the NHS has a financial stake in cleaner, filtered, air in the home. Additionally, this book proposes that dwellings should be a source of revenue as well.

There are the high rise flats and repurposed buildings (shops, warehouses, redundant office blocks etc.) to consider as well.

Today, the fundamental problem is in the price of land combined with a scarcity of homes designed for now and future needs. In addition, there is considerable volatility that makes financing the housing sector problematic.

However, the trend in inflation from houses has been with us a long time supported by a perceived shortage of homes. One can only wonder at the bright green glee in the mind's eye as we behold the property money men.

There is every incentive for a wide range of powerful institutions to keep house price inflation growing. It is an asset that keeps investors from the smallest to the biggest, happy. This is an investment in inflation not in houses. It is not an investment in assets but even so does yield an income as people pay their mortgages.

There is some evidence that the buoyant housing market in 2021 will not last, and house prices may even reduce over the next five years. Volatility also tends to drive away investors.

The prospect of future falling house prices are also politically a problem. Politicians tend not to be elected against house price instability scenarios. Taxing speculators is also a difficult option. There has to be alternatives to provide a known secure return in housing investment.

In addition, lower prices do not solve the need for accommodation; the demand for more homes will not fade even if the hyperinflation housing prices go away in the time it takes to build a housing estate.

The return we get from house price inflation is not good for the national economy. It is a case of higher prices but no productivity advantage. This need not be the case. Factory built houses cost less and are a productivity advance over bricks and mortar.

Instead of stoking inflation it is possible to turn the investment in a house into a source of income. The idea that a house can generate energy, save water, reduce public sector costs such as social care, respiratory and allergy diseases and cut public service costs such as street cleaning, grass cutting and drone postal services is an eye opener. It grows the economy and cuts public sector costs.

And, by the by, it will be quite soon when Climate Change proofed houses are in much greater demand than other homes. And with inflation capped incentive, faster house improvements that make investing in renovation and re building more attractive.

A big flood, fire, even a pandemic or social disruption caused by mass migration to avoid the effects of Climate Change with its consequential economic turmoil will have a knock on effect in the UK too.

By 2070, 19% of the world will be a barely livable hot zone. Just being outside for 4 hours will be a killer.

Less dramatic but relevant include influences like Brexit, Covid and the Ukrainian war prompting as much as 8% migration from towns and cities. The ending of the government incentives like stamp duty holidays are significant but may not be needed when as is proposed here, housing development is predicated against local need.

The Office for Budget Responsibility (OBR) in its November 2020 forecast, projected a 9% fall in house prices between the end of 2020 and the beginning of 2022. An approximation, a 1% reduction in real income has historically led to about a 2% reduction in house prices. So if incomes had fallen at the same rate as GDP, we might experience a double digit fall in prices.

High inflation and stalled economic growth are not harbingers of much more property price inflation.

The government's 95% mortgage guarantee scheme for homebuyers with 5% deposits on properties worth up to £600,000 (until the end of 2022) offers the prospect of "taking the market into overheated, dangerous territory".

These are all straws in the wind pointing to a reduction in the price of houses.

But with no let up in demand, all parts of the UK continued to report robust increases in house prices. "Respondents are pretty unanimous in once again highlighting the challenge around supply, whether in the sales or rental markets," said Simon Rubinsohn, RICS chief economist.

With demand increasing and supply continuing to falter, a net balance of 83% of surveyors reported an increase. The demand is there but prices are faltering.

The 'safe as houses' investment of home owners looks to have a much less stable future and might even be as volatile as other financial resources.

But, of course, given a chance, the Treasury Mandarins have spread our money all over the place.

The government's Clean Growth Strategy also specifically highlighted the role of local leadership: "Moving to a productive low carbon economy cannot be achieved by central government alone; it is a shared responsibility across the country. Local areas are best placed to drive emission reductions through their unique position of managing policy on land, buildings, water, waste and transport. They can embed low carbon measures in strategic plans across areas such as health and social care, transport, and housing." No mention of Climate Change.

In its 2019 manifesto, the Conservative Party pledged to spend £9.2 billion on upgrading the energy efficiency of homes, schools and hospitals. This included Social Housing.

Here then is another source of money that can be added to the renovation and renewal of dwellings.

And there are lots more:

Starting in 2022, tens of thousands of homes are to be built on derelict sites as part of a nearly £2 billion drive generously paid for by the British taxpayer through its agent, Chancellor Rishi Sunak.

There is more:

- The Decarbonisation Fund Homes is worth £3.8 billion over a ten year period.

- Home Upgrade Grants worth £2.5 billion over a five year period.

- A Public Sector Decarbonisation Scheme of £2.9 billion over a five year period.

On the 8 July 2020, Chancellor Rishi Sunak announced a £2 billion Green Homes Grant, with vouchers of up to £5,000 to help homeowners upgrade their homes, and up to £10,000 available to some of the UK's poorest families.

There is also a £1 billion programme to make public buildings, including schools and hospitals, across the UK greener and £50 million to pilot innovative approaches to retrofitting social housing at scale.

The fourth round of the Contracts for Difference (CfD) scheme which aims to secure 12GW of electricity capacity opens with £285 million a year funding for low carbon technology.

Then there is:

1. The Warm Home Discount gives £140 each year, mainly to pensioners and people who receive certain benefits. A small amount per house but a fortune overall.

2.   The Winter Fuel Payment is a payment towards your winter heating if you're aged over 66 (you get more if you're over 80).

3.   If winter is particularly cold, some households can get the £25 Cold Weather Payment for each week that it's below zero degrees.

4.   Fuel Direct can help you manage your energy bills if you get Income Support, income based Jobseeker's Allowance, income related Employment and Support Allowance, Universal Credit or Pension Credit.

Well, this is a good start, but it is only the money that can be spent. There is also a heap of money that can be saved. For example:

Building Research Establishment shows the annual costs to the NHS of poor quality and hazardous housing at £1.4 billion. This rises to £18.5 billion p.a. when wider societal costs are included (long-term care, mental health etc.).

Peter Freeman, the chairman of the government quango Homes England, reports its own investment on behalf of the government. He says "Our partners include Barclays, and Lloyds Banking Group and M&G. In March 2020, we announced a £10m investment in M&G Investments new Shared Ownership Fund. Homes England's early participation catalysed £177m of initial institutional investment, a first step towards the fund's £825m target

212

capital raised. Over the next five years the fund will develop more than 2,000 new affordable shared ownership homes in partnership with housing associations across England. This deal highlights the commitment Homes England has to supporting the growth and evolution of housing in institutional portfolios." Are such affordable homes part of new housing estates or monoculture crescents of old peoples?

Call all this money £40 billion by including savings to the NHS.

The pledges from the financial institutions have not been included and there are also Local Government funds available too.

The 2022 Queen's Speech promised even more cost to the Treasury and another attempt to add further to the current mish mash of money, regulation 'incentives' and Climate Change mitigation (and confusion with global warming).

There is more but it makes the point. There are some dwellings that are of a high standard out of the 24 million homes in the UK.

It seems that there is quite a lot of money floating around to do a stunning job and upgrade our homes against Climate Change. What is silly is that there are large sums of money cast across a lot of homes and therefore of little consequence at the sharp end. People are to a varying degree inspired by this largesse; some even do nothing at all!

There is a case for a comprehensive review of what money is being sloshed around and for what purpose.

Let's look at three examples:

First. Replace the window with heat bridge prevention, see-through solar harvesting, triple glaze performance, and a HEPA, high efficiency particulate air filter heat pump and humidity control. That would be good for a flat and something bigger for a house. In addition solar energy can be used to power the heat pump for a large part of the day.

Secondly. With average heat loss for a residence of 30% for the roof, 25% for the walls, about 7% for the floor and approximately 13% for windows and external doors, thermal, breathable insulation is a boon, not only in the winter but in summer time as well. Insulation (and there are some excellent thin insulation materials available) is important too.

Thirdly of course, energy harvesting and energy saving cladding is a revenue source from most high rise buildings and tenements. There is a payback period but solar panels on external walls are relatively efficient (and the technology is progressing fast) especially when the sun is low on the horizon during wintertime. Some walls are structurally capable for storing water too.

There are other investments that can be included in refurbishment such as electricity saving devices including light bulbs, low power washing machines and solar powered and energy creating street lights. Other forms of cost reduction that can attract funding are estate wide battery storage facilities to keep the lights on at night and offer over capacity generation to the grid or independent customers. Then there is the use of a local bottled water company selling estate harvested water. Providing automated street services such as lighting, street cleaning and grass cutting etc. has value too, and can attract funding. All these stakeholder provided services can be bundled up into a package that can be valuable investments and funded by the private sector.

The Public Private Partnership scheme whereby financial institutions fund capital assets and services are wide open to abuse and can be restructured to support the housing crisis.

Tracing the path of taxpayers, financial institutions and revenue streams in the housing sector needs to be closely managed. It needs the security and real life auditing capability of blockchain to provide immutable evidence of delivery and quality.

This could also apply to private speculative house building. What constitutes the price of new houses? Why are new houses 16% more expensive than older houses?

The next question is how does the nation get the money to where it is needed, in a timely manner?

This is where Local Authorities can come into play. They should be able to identify estates or buildings. This should be funded out of existing government funds or stakeholder cooperatives.

Within a year such applications will be monitored and financially audited using blockchain evidence (this means that central government will have built a blockchain within months, but no longer than a year to do this, using one of the existing vendors) .

Next they will inform the community stakeholders that they propose to create a local community estate to deal with Climate Change mitigation, refurbishment and renewal and then to press ahead with plans to implement the scheme.

If a neighbourhood estate is slow in its response, the local authority will be empowered to use Compulsory Purchase Orders (within a short time frame) and then engage resident's stakeholder to devise and implement a plan.

This is draconian but compared to the alternative, it is essential. This is, after all a crisis.

Not all of the needs can be delivered at once. The starting date is passed, the rate of implementation is variable and not monitored or evaluated nor sanctioned when achievement is not met.

There is no schedule of implementation except at local levels.

Perhaps there should be some targets to focus resources on the most needs. A global £5000 per household to insulate every house will mean that some are done and others next door are not. For mitigation of global warming, this is not a solution especially when a tumbledown tenement is leaking heat like a radiator and has walls running with condensation or worse.

It is going to be local authorities that will be the drivers both for prioritising need, scheduling and pressing home action. This is not to say that slum clearance and re construction are top of the list.

A street of 1970s semi's may be a better candidate for Climate Change and global warming mitigation. Most certainly, new build estates will need to adopt best practices as a matter of course and the building sector should be shamed into re building houses built in the last decade that do not meet the new standards. Or, perhaps they can be another source of income to implement Climate Change relief.

John Stewart Mills would turn in his grave at what follows.

The refurbishing of a house to meet the needs of current and the lifetime of a house/dwelling (half a century?) facing impending Climate Change will cost a lot of money.

Perhaps it can be estimated at 10% of the value of a property at current prices.

To be able to live in a house that, aside from inflation, will generate a revenue from its ability to fund a large part of the cost of living, is a big ask especially if this includes all manner of Climate Change risks.

Self-sufficient power, the cost of EV travel and transport, energy generation and storage revenues and so forth are examples of the return on investment one can envisage from Climate Change focused renovation of homes.

There are some (including Dave Elliott emeritus professor of technology policy at the Open University) who suggest that the UK will generate too much electricity within a decade and an associated balancing act to keep the lights on or off depending on the brightness of the sun and gales of wind power.

Such projections tend to beggar belief. The use of electricity generated hydrogen production to power big ships, trains, planes, lorries, iron smelting, steelworks, cement factories and even electricity generators at times renewable outages suggest there will be plenty of applications for progressively cheaper clean energy.

Replacing Russian gas and oil with British hydrogen seems to be a good deal.

We need more power not less and thereby change the dynamic of household finances.

So, there is a need to access a big capital sum to renew our ageing houses.

The average price of a house on the open market is said to be in the region of £275,000. This means that if 10% of the sale price was set aside for the renewal of property, most houses would have £27,000 available for upgrading.

What is the practicality of such an adventure?

There were over 150,000 home sales in 2021, after dramatically falling to 32,450 in May 2020 during the peak of the coronavirus (COVID 19) crisis. It is reasonable to imagine that between 15 and 20% of the housing stock is sold each year and that is a pretty good start at moving the housing stock into Climate Change mitigation in short order. This is simply a sales tax to fund what has to be done because of Climate Change.

Stop and pause for a moment after the cacophony of protest settles down. Once such a scheme was in place, the effect on the housing market and especially house prices would settle down. As for the provision of Climate Change mitigation for new dwellings, there may be a spike in house prices or even a swift reduction.

There will be those who will try to game the idea by deflating the house price and then gaining a windfall by moving the money around. A crime against Climate Change Mitigation in anyone's book. The penalty, one may wish, should come with a ten year stretch in a drafty un mitigated gaol.

Renewing and reviving 10/20% of the UK housing stock sold each year and at no cost to the public purse would be both a huge boost to the economy and employment. Furthermore, the associated ability to have distributed energy production (without the need for huge power grid cables marching over the countryside) with energy saving and nationally distributed storage (batteries) will be a boon.

Policing such an enterprise will, once again, be vested in the Professional Institutions and funded from the sales tax.

It will mean that the policy can be implemented at no cost to the treasury.

Revenue generated from second sales will be useful for adding Climate Change mitigation investment. This can be as fundamental as stormwater protection, drought alleviation, end of street power storage (long lived batteries), community mesh wifi infrastructure and so forth.

There can never be enough climate mitigation investment in the home and in the community and a house sale tax will be a worthwhile solution.

It is possible to resolve the Housing Crisis and mitigate the effects of Climate Change.

Sources and References

Green Finance Institute,
https://www.greenfinanceinstitute.co.uk/. Accessed 12 May
2022.

"• Average house price in the UK 2007 2022." Statista, 13
April 2022,
https://www.statista.com/statistics/751605/average house
price in the uk/. Accessed 13 May 2022.

"Biggest ever renewable energy support scheme opens."
GOV.UK, 13 December 2021,
https://www.gov.uk/government/news/biggest ever
renewable energy support scheme opens. Accessed 12 May
2022.

"Biggest ever renewable energy support scheme opens."
GOV.UK, 13 December 2021,
https://www.gov.uk/government/news/biggest ever
renewable energy support scheme opens. Accessed 12 May
2022.

"Bottled drinking water: how to produce and label."
GOV.UK, 28 May 2020,
https://www.gov.uk/guidance/bottled drinking water how to
produce and label. Accessed 12 May 2022.

Boyce, Lee. "New build homes cost 16% more than
existing ones, LCPa index reveals." This is Money
(UK), 1 May 2018,

https://www.thisismoney.co.uk/money/mortgageshome/arti cle 5674423/New build homes cost 16 existing properties LCPa index reveals.html. Accessed 12 May 2022.

Clover, Ian, and Blake Matich. "UK solar leaders launch comprehensive commercial rooftop PV guide." PV Magazine, 20 July 2016, https://www.pv magazine.com/2016/07/20/uk solar leaders launch comprehensive commercial rooftop pv guide_100025495/. Accessed 12 May 2022.

Cottrell, Anna. "UK house prices will crash, experts say – here's when it will happen." Ideal Home, 8 June 2021, https://www.idealhome.co.uk/news/property experts predicting a house price crash 278213. Accessed 12 May 2022.

"Deadly heat waves projected in the densely populated agricultural regions of South Asia." PubMed, 2 August 2017, https://pubmed.ncbi.nlm.nih.gov/28782036/. Accessed 12 May 2022.

Elliott, Dave. "Too much of a good thing: an excess of UK renewables? – Physics World." Physics World, 31 October 2018, https://physicsworld.com/a/too much of a good thing an excess of uk renewables/. Accessed 13 May 2022.

"Government Energy Grants For Your Home Which?" Which? Magazine, https://www.which.co.uk/reviews/home

grants/article/home grants/government energy grants for your home avOaP8E1ZGdx. Accessed 12 May 2022.

Hammond, George. "What London's falling population means for the housing market." Financial Times, 21 January 2021, https://www.ft.com/content/517ff59b 16a4 4412 9798 d06268771797. Accessed 12 May 2022.

Hockaday, James. "Britain's most depressing high street revealed as record number of shops close." Metro, 10 April 2019, https://metro.co.uk/2019/04/10/britains most depressing high street revealed with record numbers of shops closing 9149690/. Accessed 12 May 2022.

Holley, Eamon. "Public Private Partnerships in the United Kingdom." Lexology, 26 March 2019, https://www.lexology.com/library/detail.aspx?g=18fc6332 5ad1 4b5d b69c 8b47d308bd99. Accessed 12 May 2022.

"House prices set to continue rising as supply shrinks." BBC, 8 July 2021,https://www.bbc.co.uk/news/business 57754558. Accessed 12 May 2022.

"Housing prices in the UK and London fall, homelessness rises, more children than ever sleep in B&Bs – Danny Dorling." Danny Dorling, https://www.dannydorling.org/?p=6407. Accessed 12 May 2022.

Jones, Rupert. "Value of UK house sales forecast to leap 46% this year as boom continues." The Guardian, 25 May 2021, https://www.theguardian.com/business/2021/may/26/value of uk house sales forecast to leap 46 this year as boom continues. Accessed 12 May 2022.

"London property market risk and financial services." ICAEW, https://www.icaew.com/technical/financial services/2021/london property market risk and financial services. Accessed 12 May 2022.

Meen, Geoffrey, and Christine Whitehead. "Understanding Affordability The Economics of Housing Markets, By Geoffrey Meen and Christine Whitehead." Bristol University Press, https://bristoluniversitypress.co.uk/understanding affordability. Accessed 12 May 2022.

Pettifor, Ann. "Why building more homes will not solve Britain's housing crisis | Ann Pettifor." The Guardian, 27 January 2018, https://www.theguardian.com/commentisfree/2018/jan/27/b uilding homes britain housing crisis?CMP=share_btn_tw. Accessed 12 May 2022.

"Queen's Speech 2022." GOV.UK, 10 May 2022, https://www.gov.uk/government/speeches/queens

speech 2022. Accessed 13 May 2022.

"Solar Panel Grants." Warma UK,
https://warmauk.com/solar panel grants/. Accessed 12 May
2022.

Chapter 10: Beurocratic Rubble Swept Away

This book has covered a wide range of issues. Its referencing points to many sources which support claims that have been made which lead to a number of conclusions.

It is a policy statement for both parliamentarians and government institutions. Here too are planning activities that can help local authorities and parish councils. The professions have a stake in this publication as well as do many other members of the public.

Now we look at a summary of the findings without much of the detailed criticism above.

There are three crises facing us and our political masters. Global Warming, Climate Change and the lack of suitable housing. They are distinct but also interlinked.

The rate at which these three issues are changing is accelerating.

Heating, cooling and powering existing offices, homes and factories account for 27% of global energy-related carbon-dioxide emissions. By one estimate, cities will need to add 13,000 buildings every day until 2050, just to keep up with global population growth.

Government is not grasping the significance of the extent and rate of change despite the evidence in national and global news coverage and the raft of scientific evidence.

The number of houses and the different forms of housing is a big issue. House price inflation, demand for more and more houses and the need to make houses Climate Change mitigated is not being faced.

There is also an issue with building homes to meet local needs. Much of British housing is built speculatively to the chagrin of local communities.

The way we live is already changing. Already robots cut lawns, solar panels provide free fuel for our cars and phones switch on the sitting room lights from across the world using mobile phone apps. The income a house can generate by harvesting energy and generating hydrogen is quite remarkable. Furthermore, the cost of running a properly insulated and heated building can be cut in half or better. The cost of power for a car should be pennies and home must be a healthy place to live.

Soon computer games will escape nine-year-olds and the estate wide wifi service and will let grown-ups enjoy metaverse meals with friends all over time zones.

Of course, being able to resolve housing and Climate Change crises, and the ability to plan and manage developments is a challenge. Building houses in rain and wind is silly when they can be built in the warmth of a modern factory. With dwellings designed to maximise the amount of renewable power they produce and offer fast and nationally distributed power generation growth and storage is a boon.

The need for huge ugly solar farms will vanish as the roofs of 300,000 new houses built every year come on stream with new solar power. The nature of distributed resources serves to protect the nation from massive infrastructure failure and can be archived rapidly.

There is another element to all of this. There are many institutions that represent whole industries. They have, in the past been given Charters and privileges for their members. They claim to educate members and ensure the best possible practice.

Now, though, it's time for them to monitor the quality and modernity of their members and their members' work. They need sanctions against those who fail and should they fail there is a need for sanctions against them and their membership. In this way, much of the cost of government can be eliminated and will be born by the members of these mighty institutions.

Being able to optimise the opportunities available for tomorrow's living, there is a need to be able to invite homeowners and other stakeholders to cooperate. They need to be able to maintain their local environment and take away many of the costly tasks local government in particular undertake. Local communities will have to cooperate in many ways to save costs and to maintain Climate Change environments.

Grass cutting, street lighting and providing high-quality internet connectivity are good examples but so too are facilities to maximise and provide nationally distributed storage and commercial value of estate-wide batteries, a faster and environmentally better option than huge battery farms.

Building houses that, at the same time, address issues of global warming, Climate Change and there need for more homes is something of a problem in the present circumstances.

Of course, factory-built homes are a self-evident need. They will have to be of high quality and built to standards to meet the needs of an environment changing faster than most acknowledge. There are some simple actions that are of national importance. Properly filtered air cuts out a lot of the pollution, viruses and pollen. Such a simple thing will save the NHS millions of pounds every year. Equally, there is a need for space to live in. The charity Mind makes it quite clear that limited living space affects mental health and is a cost to the NHS and not having somewhere to put a bike or